Advaita Vedanta
for
Ordinary People

Stephan Kahlert

Publisher: Inspiring Publishers,
P.O. Box 159, Calwell, ACT Australia 2905
Email: publishaspg@gmail.com
http://www.inspiringpublishers.com

A catalogue record for this
book is available from the
NATIONAL
LIBRARY   National Library of Australia
OF AUSTRALIA

National Library of Australia The Prepublication Data Service

Author: Stephan Kahlert
Title: Advaita Vedanta for Ordinary People
Genre: Non-fiction, Mind Body and Spirit / Yoga
ISBN: 978-1-925908-04-6

"To bring across the fundamental ideas of Advaita Vedanta for Ordinary People in an easy to understand format is not easy. I really liked the way Stephan Kahlert (Pujan) brings these ancient teachings alive in his book, making it understandable to western readers. It is full of personal stories and it is easy to read. I've know him for many years, and it is a joy to hear him teach."

- Dr. Satyam Gopalan,
CFO at Global Watch Foundation Children's Home,
Founder at Sunshine Guest House in India,
Manages Edesia Nashville

An unexamined life is not worth living. Everyone suffers a sometimes crippling sense of limitation as they wend their way through this uncertain world, but it need not be that way. This introduction to Vedanta by Stephen Kahlert, presents a proven solution to suffering in a simple straightforward way that anyone who is sincerely committed to answering the perennial existential question, "Who am I really?" can understand.   Stephan's whole adult life has been devoted to the quest for freedom and, with the help of Vedanta, has laid to rest this fundamental doubt."

James Swartz

"Brahman is real
The world is only apparently real
You as an individual self are nothing other than Brahman."

- Shri Shankaracharya

I dedicate this book to all "Seekers"
so they become "Finders."

Acknowledgments

Without the constant support of my friend Sole, who patiently sat with me discussing all the complex spiritual issues, this book would not have seen the light. The beautiful drawings at the end are all her creativity, and I am so thankful that she helped me with the work.

I want to thank Indica Jehman (Satya) who encouraged me to continue writing and gave me great feedback. She did the editing work on the book. I never knew that writing a book is so complex.

And, of course, Betty Kah, my wife and constant support through all my life.

And, last not least, my inspiration and teacher James Swartz and his wife Sundari, who introduced me to the non-dual path of Vedanta.

I bow down in deep gratitude to all of you.

Hari Om Tat Sat.

Table of Contents

Introduction

Since childhood I had the feeling that there must be more to life. I watched my parents, who survived the Second World War, and who were happy to work hard to fulfill their dream of having material wealth and a roof over their heads.

I was born in Germany in the 50s at a time that was dominated by what the Germans called "wiederaufbau." Translation: Built it again! Material wealth came back and the whole country was striving to get ahead.

I remember once I saw an advertising from a bank that read "Work till 65 and then live!" They were pointing to the retirement age, apparently the time to start living. But what about now? My spiritual search began at this point.

What is the meaning of my life? Does life even have a meaning? Is there a God or is everything just by chance? How to live and to love in a meaningful way?

The questioning went on and on and after being involved as a protestant, the religion of my birth, I soon looked for answers in eastern religions.

At this time I was studying psychology, and up to this point I only knew what neurotic behavior was and how to approach it.

In my studies I did not come across an explanation of what a "healthy human being" was. Eastern Philosophy pointed to a realization of Oneness that they called enlightenment, referring to a permanent freedom and a solid, grounded happiness.

Yes, this is what I want!

If you understand what I'm describing, this book is for you.

It took me nearly 25 years of being a "seeker" to finally arrive at Advaita Vedanta. I am not saying that Vedanta is the only way, but once you have certain qualifications to understand the basic underlining truth, you will be able to realize your true nature. And then, most likely, burst out laughing because the truth is so obvious, once you know it.

Why is this book for "ordinary" people?

With the word "ordinary" I want to point out that the truth is simple and ordinary. You don't need to be "special."

The Truth (the Self) is difficult to perceive and understand when your mind is confused and drawn to either very esoteric explanations or very emotional justifications.

The truth of who you are is right here, but we are so busy looking elsewhere.

We are hoping that a teacher can "give us" the truth. Or some drugs can reveal the truth for us. These substances can perhaps help sometimes, but are we able to understand what is happening to us?

Sometimes, just being in a special place can help us to forget our worries.

That brings me to my second point: this is not a self-help book. Self-help is a self-guided improvement. It can be economical, intellectual or emotional. It often has a substantial psychological basis.

However Vedanta is not based on psychology, even though psychology and Vedanta have similarities. In the last few years the gap between these two practices of inquiry has become smaller, but considerable differences still exist.

When I was first introduced to Advaita Vedanta, I had already searched for many, many years. The "spiritual market place" was well known to me.

My search began with Osho in India. His teachings were exactly what I needed at that time. Not serious spiritual discourses, but a party-like atmosphere, with psychological and religious influences. It opened me up to a different world and I became a more receptive and sensitive being. He introduced me to meditation, and later I was pulled into a more Buddhist-based meditative practice. When he died in 1990 I was without a spiritual guide, and so I looked for alternatives.

My journey was similar to many of Osho's followers: I went to Lucknow, India to sit with a teacher by the name of Papaji. He had no teaching, but yet to sit in his presence was divine. However this was not enough for me! I was hungry for a teaching that was more than a "feel good" feeling. So I kept on searching.

Through Papaji I opened myself to Advaita teachers like Robert Adams and Nisargadatta Maharaj. Both were pointing in the right direction, but how do I get there? Both were talking from their own experience so it was difficult for me to find practical instructions that I could actually follow.

My search ended when I found my teacher James Swartz - or Ramji, as we call him.

Finally I found logic in the search. I've had enough of suggestions like I should "just let go" or to "open my heart" or to "just be" or even to "be here now." This did not make any sense to me and left me even more confused.

It was the teaching of the Upanishads that explained what is real (Satya) and what is apparently real (Mithya). Just understanding this discrimination was the beginning of a whole new world to me. Suddenly this whole spiritual search became not only an emotional journey, but it also became unemotionally, clear and real.

Now Vedanta is much more in fashion and teachers are throwing Vedantic concepts around and mixing them with their own ideas.

Where I live, on a tropical Thai island, there are teachers who claim that tantra and Vedanta are interchangeable, and many more unclear versions of it.

There is also confusion with Hatha Yoga.

I have taught yoga teacher trainings for over 14 years. My challenge is to introduce yoga philosophy subtly into the program. A standard form of philosophy teaching is the Patanjali Yoga Sutras. These sutras are highly specific, difficult to follow, and are based on Samkhya, a dualistic yoga path.

Very often the non-dual path of Advaita Vedanta is thrown into the mix by teachers who cannot differentiate the traditions. Therefore the knowledge of Advaita Vedanta is not understood correctly.

When Ramji wrote "The Essence of Enlightenment " I thought that it was a book that explained Advaita Vedanta methodically, and that everybody would understand it.

As a teacher, I realized that there is room for an easier version of Advaita Vedanta.

It is not simple to write about something complex and highly technical in an "easy to digest" format. In this process I had to drop a few important Vedantic concepts, like the role of Maya and Ishvara for example.

Sometimes my choice of words are not correct interpretations of Advaita, but this was the compromise I had to take in order to make this teaching more accessible. I used repetition as a necessary tool to deepen these complex teachings. Hearing these concepts again and again will help you.

The difficulty in using words in Advaita Vedanta is that words, by their very nature, are dual. Hot does not make any sense if you don't know cold. Advaita Vedanta is non-dual, there is no "other." When we talk from Mithya, the apparent reality, then words make sense. When we try to explain the unchanging, uncreated and limitless reality of the Self, then words can be misleading.

I want to make it very clear from the beginning that I don't claim to be a Vedanta scholar. What is written in this book contains my own limited understanding. If this creates confusion in you, it will be my own inability to explain the teaching correctly, not the flaw of the teaching.

If you like what you are reading and want to know more about Vedanta, please go to the site of my teacher:

http://www.shiningworld.com.

I am always open to your feedback:

swpujan@gmail.com or www.pujanyoga.com.

1

VEDANTA FUNDAMENTALS

When you enter a new environment, like a new country for instance, it is important that you either learn the language or at least have a map that shows you where you are and what will be ahead of you.

The same is when you first start to explore Vedanta.

In Zen culture, they say you have to have a beginner's mind. There is a story to illustrate this idea:

A philosophy professor visits a Zen Master. The professor comes in and starts asking questions straight away, but the Master interrupts him and says: "Wait, let's have a cup of tea first."

Japan, with its Zen culture, is unique in that it creates a meditation out of very ordinary daily activities like gardening, flower arrangements, painting, or drinking a cup of tea. A tea ceremony can take a long time, from waiting for the water to boil in silence, the warming up of the teapot, to whisking the powdered tea.

The professor was very impatient waiting to ask his question. Finally the Master came over and poured the tea into the small teacup. He poured and poured till the tea was over flowing the cup. "Stop" the professor said. "My tea cup is full, it is overflowing, can't you see that? " The Master smiled and said. "Yes, I can see you are overflowing with questions, but unless you can empty your cup from all you think you know, you will not be able to receive what I am about to teach you."

This is also very true for receiving the teaching of Vedanta.

Sravana, Manana and Nididhyasana

In Vedanta we have three steps to absorb the teaching.

Sravana (Listening)

Sravana refers to listening to the new knowledge with an open mind. A mind that can receive the teaching as it is explained by a qualified teacher. At the beginning, you are asked to put your old understanding on hold in order to absorb this new knowledge.

In the Panchadasi text it is said that "Sravana without meditation is like adding sugar to tea without stirring." Meditation will prepare the mind to receive the teaching.

Sometimes what you hear is counterintuitive and far away from your everyday understanding, so you need to trust in the teacher and in the teaching to accept this new knowledge, trying not to push it right out of your mind.

Quite often something else happens that I observed in new seekers. Their mind tells them that "I know that already...the world is all one...I just have to be...there is nothing to do..." and so on.

These are popular themes in Neo Advaita Vedanta, which is a new hybrid form of Vedanta. They have no teaching as such, but just an emphasis on the non-dual nature of reality, without a clear path to "get" there.

Just listen to the unfolding of the teaching with an open mind, and let the teaching do its work.

If you are qualified, the Self will understand this new knowledge and celebrate. (Qualifications will be explained in chapter four.)

Manana (Reflecting)

Manana refers to reflecting on the teaching. Now you reflect on the old understanding that you put on hold at the beginning (Sravana).

Whatever does not fit anymore in the light of your new understanding, you let go. Now, the new insight and knowledge that you gained will dissolve your old assumptions about the nature of reality.

Depending how hardwired ignorance is, this might take some time. Ignorance (avidya) in Vedanta refers to not knowing that you are the uncreated, non-dual, actionless, and ordinary Awareness.

Nididhyasana (Assimilation)

Nididhyasana refers to the assimilation of the knowledge. It is like "walking your talk."

Are you able to discriminate what is real (Satya) from what is apparently real (mithya)?

Can you bring this new understanding into your life and back up your knowledge with your experience?

Can you purify yourself to the point that the teaching will transform you and you will finally realize the Truth of who you really are?

At this stage you know that you are the Self but your knowledge is not firm, so constant application of the non-dual teaching is necessary.

In your everyday life you need to become brutally honest and real with yourself and bring light into your unconscious interactions with people and situations. Nididhyasana has to be applied 24/7 in order to overcome deep rooted ignorance.

In the Bhagavad Gita it says that no effort on the spiritual path will ever be lost. A comforting thought for many!

Nididhyasana might take a few years. It will be a constant reflection, a studying of Vedantic scriptures, sharing your insight with others seekers, and once in a while, with a teacher.

The tradition promises that once you practice nididhyasana, you can relax, it will bring you to Self-realization.

My teacher used the analogy of being on the Vedanta bus. We can put down our "luggage" because once we understand the teaching, we will get to the final destination sooner or later.

Of course, the truth is that liberation is not somewhere else, but already our reality. Words are not often the best way to explain spiritual truths because language, by its very nature, is dualistic. However the Truth, according to the scriptures and confirmed by yogis, is non-dual.

At best, it can be a "finger pointing to the moon." Let us not discuss about the finger but rather let's raise our head and look where the finger is pointing to.

When we are talking about this knowledge this refers to "Advaita Vedanta." Advaita meaning "not two." This indicates the oneness of Existence.

"Veda " and " anta " (Vedanta) means " the end of the Vedas." The Upanishads appear at the end of the Vedas and they also represent the highest wisdom.

Advaita Vedanta and Upanishads

There are four very old venerable scriptures called the Vedas. Some estimate that the oldest one, the Rig Veda, is over 4, 000 years old. The age of these scriptures does not really matter so much, it is their content that matters!

We are not so concerned about the Vedas because they mostly deal with how to balance your life in harmony with the laws of nature. They are full of descriptions of what mantras to chant and when or what ritual to prepare. They are mainly the duties of Hindu priests known as Brahmins, who study them. They also serve for the material well-being of society.

We are more interested in the sections that follow each Veda, known as the Upanishads, which were added later. The strict translation of Upanishad means "sitting at the foot of the teacher" and that's how the teachings have been taught.

I remember a sadhu in India who told me after we had shared some time together: "Now find a good tree in your home country to sit under and teach!" In a way I am still doing that, but of course only sometimes literally.

Shri Adi Shankara, a saint who made Vedanta very popular in India in the 8th century, said that Upanishad means Atma Vidya (the knowledge of the Self) or Brahma Vidya (the knowledge of Brahma). In any case, the Upanishads teach the highest wisdom and so they end the Vedas.

They are around 108 collected scriptures that are classified as the Upanishads, but it is believed that many must have been lost over the centuries. Even to this day some saints can add to the vast knowledge of Vedanta, and it has been said that there are now 200 Upanishads recognized in total.

These texts are lectures given to students by enlightened beings known as jnanis. Vedanta has three main sources of teaching: the Upanishads, the Brahma Sutras, and the Bhagavad Gita. All of these teachings are very dense and not easy to understand, so there are many commentaries about these texts to help students.

The Upanishads are mostly conversations between a teacher and a student, and often start with the question, "Who Am I?" or a similar "flavor." The teachings are all based on some fundamental ideas that are important for you, the reader, to understand. I will make references to these scriptures all the time and to some Sanskrit terms as well, so please stay with me.

Firstly, it is important to understand why the Upanishads and their wisdom differs from other sacred texts. They are called "shruti," which means, "I have heard" and it indicates that this wisdom is not cooked up by humans because, as my teacher said, "humans always have an agenda."

Ok, relax, we don't say that it came from aliens!

It is an indication that the knowledge is so "out of the normal perception" for human beings, that it must have come from the collective consciousness. This truth cannot be perceived with your five senses, and even inference will not do. For example, the assumption that when there is smoke there must be a fire will not work here.

The understanding of non-dual Vedanta is counterintuitive, but your own experience can back it up.

It reminds me of a story about Einstein. He was working on the relativity theory and he could not solve it, even though he tried hard. He gave up and had a long, long bath. He totally relaxed, maybe played with bubbles and a duck, when suddenly the answer to the problem exploded in him. He found the formula for the relativity theory: e=mc2.

Even though he spent years thinking and analyzing the theory of relativity, the solution only came once his mind became still. Not through thinking more about it was it solved, but through "something else." And interestingly, at the same time, a few other scientists were very close to the same discovery with no connection to Einstein. He got the first insight and then all the other mathematicians had the formula and could solve the puzzle.

Do you remember the story of Archimedes? He relaxed in his bathtub and found the mathematical formula of how to assess the purity of gold. He ran out naked and screamed, "Eureka, Eureka!" meaning "I got it, I got it." This knowledge came to him.

Back to Vedanta, what is so totally strange and counterintuitive?

That life is non-dual, and You (the Self) are it.

Yes, what you perceive with your senses is only apparently real.

We need to define what is real:

THAT WHICH NEVER CHANGES.

What never changes?

The only one thing that fits that category is YOUR AWARENESS (You).

We can call it Consciousness, but with that word there can be confusion as in super consciousness, altered consciousness, and so on.

There is only one Consciousness: Awareness, that shines like a sun onto our three bodies, which are only apparently real. (We will refer to the word Awareness in this book.)

Our Three Bodies of Consciousness

In Vedanta we talk about the existence of three bodies of consciousness.

The Gross Body

The Gross Body is composed of the five elements: Earth, Water, Fire, Air and Ether, as well as the five senses, which relate to these five elements.

Earth is related to the sense of smell and so it has its connection in our bodies through the nose.

Water is related to the sense of taste and so its connection with the body is the tongue.

Fire is related to seeing and it's connected to our eyes.

Air is related to feeling and sensations and is connected to touch.

Ether, the most subtle of the elements, is connected to hearing and the ears.

The Subtle Body

This body has three parts:

Manas - (I feel), indicating what we understand as our mind, feelings, and emotions.

Ahamkara - (I want) or what we call in the west our ego. It is the apparent doer and enjoyer in us that wants things done here and now.

Buddhi - (I think), our intellect, the part in us that learns and holds information.

How do they all work together?

The information that comes from our senses will get first sorted by our mind (manas). Have you ever wondered why you are not flooded with sensory information? All your senses are working with the same receptivity. You smell, taste, see, sense, and hear all the time! Only what you "think" is important at the moment will be recognized by you.

When you read this, your eyes will take most of your attention so you won't be able to perceive subtle sounds and smells, subtle sensations on your skin, or any tastes in your mouth. The portion of your subtle body called manas is focusing on what is important for you in this moment.

There are more examples of how the three parts of the subtle body work together.

I often tell the story of the cookie monster, a popular figure in the children's show known as Sesame Street. This cookie monster walks around and suddenly smells cookies. His manas (mind) is triggered by smell and the smell triggers feelings of the last time he ate some. His ahamkara (his doer, ego, enjoyer) comes in, the active part, which wants to have it now.

If there is not a strong buddhi (intellect), like with the cookie monster, it will run and eat all the cookies without thinking. With a trained intellect, he may consider if that is the right thing to do; how many cookies he had already today; and if he has enough money to buy them, and so on.

This example shows how the intellect is the controlling part in the subtle body and the direct link to the causal body (which we will discuss later). The good news is that you can train your intellect with knowledge.

Every living being, including plants and animals, have consciousness and a subtle body. Of course, in plants the subtle body is very rudimentary. When the sun shines, plants turn to the light and respond in opening their petals towards the sun. Scientists can even measure that plants feel a certain joy when bees start to pollinate them.

Animals have a more developed subtle body. The idea, very popular when I was in my 20s, that dolphins are more intelligent than humans, dogs and apes - is not true. It is a blessing that they don't brood about the meaning of their existence, discussing it with other animals, and don't become frustrated or depressed when they don't have an answer!

When we learn anything it will be through our intellect.

Does that mean we have an objective clear mind?

Do we have a mind that observes the information received by our senses as they arise and draws the right information from it?

Unfortunately no!

The Causal Body

Our intellect is influenced by our casual body. The name comes from the natural law of cause and effect. The causal body "causes" our subtle body to act. Remember that our "acting part" (the doer) is the ahamkara (the ego).

We can experience the gross body (physical body) and the subtle body (conscious mind), but we are not able to experience the causal body (subconscious mind).

The Causal Body has two parts: vasanas and gunas.

What are Vasanas?

Vasanas are subconscious imprints that we create through every act we do. Every activity leaves a subtle "fragrance" in our subtle body.

If you imagine a pure white sugar cone and you drop just one drop of water on the top, where will it go? Nobody knows, it can trickle randomly down the cone and create a little path. The next drop can follow an unpredictable course, but the chance that it follows the first drop is high. With the third and fourth drops, the certainty gets stronger. Every time the groove deepens.

Here is another example that I found out when I lived in a community in Australia:

There were beautiful, slightly sloped, grassy farmlands. When you first let the cows into the paddock, it was random where they will go down the hill. One cow leads and all the others follow. The second time, the leading cow would choose exactly the same route and the path will trample down, creating a small trail that all the cows follow. When it starts to rain, the water would follow the created trail and deepen it, eroding the land.

This should give you an idea of how vasanas are originated. Deeper imprints in our causal body are called samskaras.

Every like and dislike creates a vasana. Every fearful response, every act of greed, or every hateful thought will create a vasana (an imprint in your mind).

There are also vasanas that Buddhists would call "skillful," like the routine of getting up early to do yoga or meditate, eating healthy food, or reading spiritual texts.

Vasanas are our accumulated likes and dislikes that have a substantial subconscious influence on our "supposedly" free actions. In fact, they color every action we do.

How do we neutralize them?

How do we lessen their impact on our life and be more spontaneous and fearless?

In some cases, therapy will help make these vasanas (known as hard-wired patterns and tendencies in psychology) more clear to you, and it will become easier to recognize them when they arise.

Once you see and feel they are arising, you have to neutralize them by not giving them your attention.

Every action creates a vasana, so the way you react will determine if a vasana gets stronger or weaker.

Sometimes it is enough to produce an opposite thought to balance out a vasana. Sometimes it needs both a strong action and a change of attitude towards the situation. A popular description would be "deconditioning" your actions and your thoughts.

There is one more factor that will influence us, and these are the gunas. When I first looked into Vedanta, and particularly into the Bhagavad Gita, I had not heard about the gunas. I was following a Zen Buddhist path, and to my knowledge there was no mention of the gunas there. But once I understood what the gunas were, I found them invaluable in understanding my emotional side.

In the 70s there was no recognition of the gunas in the study of psychology. It was all explained away by hormonal fluctuations and unconscious memories that were accumulated in your childhood. Understanding the functioning of the gunas makes me a much better psychologist.

2

THE GUNAS

The gunas are qualities that "bind" us to consciousness, facilitating the assimilation of experiences.

There are three gunas: tamas, which can be compared to an iron chain; rajas is more like a silver chain; and sattva is like a golden chain.

The gunas are a clear definition of the three "energies" or "qualities" that run the universe, including my personal life and yours. These three kinds of global universal experiences are known and common to everyone, but were hardly ever singled out and explained.

We have:

1. The feeling of activity (rajas).
2. The feeling of inertia (tamas).
3. The feeling of happiness without a reason (sattva).

We can generally say that rajas is a busy mind that wants to "do" and achieve all the time, and is over confident.

Tamas is pretty much the opposite, a negative, dull and lazy haze.

Sattva is that feeling of "being in the zone." A state that is more and more recognized in the modern world as a desirable place to be. Clear, calm, and centered.

Let's analyze them in more detail:

Rajas

Rajas is the energy of the ego (ahamkara) and its qualities are ambition, busyness, being "on the go," and a very active mind. I am sure we all are familiar with that. This is the guna our western society runs off, and increasingly in the east as well.

The food that supports rajas is of course fast food, and especially spicy food, and food that can be ideally eaten while walking around. What is the favorite beverage of rajasic people? Coffee, the new hybrid Red Bull, and other high-powered energy drinks.

When I first moved to Australia in 1978 the common drink was tea. Not just a tea bag, but the whole ritual that involved a "cuppa," as the Australians called it. This included boiling the water on the stove; cleaning the tea pot with hot water; throwing tea leaves in; turning the pot three times to the right and left; after three minutes getting a sieve out; pouring the tea in individual cups; adding sugar and milk; waiting a bit more. And finally, slowly sipping it.

It took a long time - time that was used to talk, share and connect. It was normal to have spontaneous meetings on the weekends where you just "popped in" to see your friends while sipping on tea.

In Germany during my student years, it was typical for friends to come over on a weekend morning with bread rolls and we would sit and talk until late afternoon. Try to do that today! With a few exceptions, we have become so busy that even using social media, it is hard to meet up - and impossible to spontaneously connect. Rajas runs our life.

Rajas is the mode of passion and it pushes us to activities. When rajas takes over our intellect, we want to feel that life is forward-looking. We are goal-oriented and we want results very badly. If we don't get what we want, we feel frustrated.

We don't understand that we have no control over the outcome of any action. The Whole, Ishvara, God, the Buddha field, the Dharma field - or whatever you believe that keeps the world spinning - has the control.

Emotional people are very happy when they get what they want, and they are very depressed if they don't get what they want. They are attached to the idea that they always need to do some activity that can lead to naive actions. Their mind is constantly agitated and they cannot act deliberately or skillfully. As a result, they experience boredom and suffer. They are victims of doership, not realizing that the gunas, and in this case - rajas, are the doers.

With rajas the problem is inflation and deflation. When you get what you want, you get an exaggerated sense of self-importance. When you don't get what you want, you get a sense of failure and depression. Rajasic people are too busy acting out their desires without reflecting on the results of their actions.

This famous quote explains rajas well: "The definition of insanity is doing the same thing again and again and expecting different results." (Albert Einstein)

Rajasic people are very stubborn and defensive. They are in constant conflict with the world.

The biggest problem in our western society is how to deal with stress and the consequences of burn out (heart attacks, anxiety, etc,). These are the side effects of rajas.

The dynamic lifestyle that a rajasic person is acting out happens when they get what they desire. When the universe does not deliver, tamas takes over!

Tamas

Tamas is the most destructive energy of the three gunas. Its qualities are inertia, dullness, fogginess, and laziness.

Tamasic people like to watch rather than to do. For example, tamasic thinking is wanting to go for the "easy money" rather than work for it (rajas).

I remember when my son was around 13-years-old, a time when all teenagers can be quite tamasic if they are left to their own devices. When the doorbell rang and a friend of my son's came in - without him or me saying anything - I pointed to the room and I observed when he entered. Without my son even saying much, he pointed to the Play Station and they both proceeded to play video games for hours. This is a form of real tamasic-passive entertainment.

When they were hungry, what do you think they wanted to eat? A fresh salad and a healthy juice, or a cheese pizza with a bottle of coke? The greasy tamasic food always won. Of course heavy, oily food makes you even more tamasic.

In adults, tamas leads to sensuality and a pursuit of short-term pleasures like alcohol, drugs and over eating. It encourages a lazy way of thinking "out of sight, out of mind." There is no long-term evaluation of the consequences of their actions - just quick fixes and instant gratifications of food, sleeping, sex, and other short-term goals. The karma they are creating is mostly "negative karma," meaning that they often are in debt - financially and energetically.

Life for a tamasic person is always a burden and a big weight on their shoulders. They don't grow, they are messy, forgetful, and prone to accidents and losses of many kinds. They are mostly confused, with a sense of failure. Energy never stands still, it either moves upwards or spirals downwards, often leading to depression.

The two energies of tamas and rajas are like terrible twins. They are always coming together.

How do you get out of tamas? By using some rajasic methods.

Be aware when tamas, in the form of laziness, descends on you and then act!

Sometimes you just need to move your body in a vigorous way, doing any kind of physical exercise like yoga, jogging, trekking, swimming, etc. A cold shower or jumping into the ocean is another great way to transform tamas into rajas. Anything that keeps your heart pumping will help.

Simultaneously, be aware of what you put into your mouth. Heavy greasy food will pull you down into tamas, just like roping a heavy stone around your legs.

Of course that sounds so simple, but like all changes, it is not easy to do. It is even more difficult to get out of rajas. When we are in tamas, on a deeper level, we know that this is not helpful or productive and creative, but being in rajas can often feel right!

Certainly even tamas has its place. For example, when you need to go to sleep or when you need to "ground" your emotions.

Rajas often feels right because, as we established earlier, western society is built on rajasic values. We don't see that aimless rushing around, multi-tasking, or trying to be at two places at once will not make us more productive. This builds up anxiety and feeds an already busy mind.

How to slow down?

The first thing to do is to become aware that rajas is controlling you.

This is often not easy if somebody else tries to do that for you. When my wife rushes around the room trying to do many things at the same time and gets annoyed because she can't find the car keys she just had in her hand, for me to remind her by saying, "Darling, just breathe" could trigger another explosion!

An example is shown in a Zen story where a student came to his master and proclaimed his enlightenment. The master looked at him and asked, "Good, but now tell me where did you put your shoes when you came in?" The student was confused and could not recall what happened to his shoes. "Go back and meditate some more, unless you can bring all your attention to every single moment, you are not ready."

The transformation from rajas into sattva can be very quick once you become aware of which guna you are in. Just stopping and consciously breathing: in, out, in, out - will bring you back. Then, you might decide to stop for a cup of tea and just let the world drift by. Becoming more aware is always the key for changing behavior.

I worked as a business consultant for a while. One associate told me that they persuaded a big bank to create rooms for contemplation. A place where executives were encouraged to sit for 10 to 20 minutes just to be still for a while, relax, and ground themselves - before they start another meeting. No phones or computers were allowed. There was strict silence and the room had no decorations of any kind. The results were very promising, as the meetings became much shorter, conflicts went down, and money was saved. (Of course the bottom line in any business!) This is an example of balancing rajas, so that sattva can arise.

Sattva

Sattva is an experience of deep contentment without any reason. A feeling of clarity and fullness where nothing can be added or taken away.

It happens to all of us, but we are often not aware of it arising and disappearing. Suddenly, let's say after a yoga class, you feel wonderful and the world is in total harmony. Or you see a beautiful sunset, or you just stop for a moment and look out of your window and feel peace. Mostly these moments don't last long. The phone rings or "urgent" thoughts and commitments arise and pull you back into rajas.

Once back in rajas, the memory of sattva pushes you to try to bring clarity back again and again. This is a noble move because only from sattva we can easily recognize our true nature (Satya).

There is another hidden risk that is unique to sattva that happens to a lot of spiritual people. When they commit themselves to a yogic lifestyle, their ego comes in and starts judging others. I lived most of my life in so-called "spiritual" places and I saw this happening a lot.

I remember sharing with some friends that I was a vegetarian for the past 25 years (by the way, I am not strict anymore). I was happy with my diet. The vegan next to me was disappointed because I still used animal products like dairy, eggs and honey. In his opinion, as a spiritual person, I should not do that. Then, the raw food eater who sat at the table as well, claimed that cooking any food would kill all the nutrients and that we both should come to a deeper understanding if we really wanted to be healthy and spiritual.

There are many other examples of the same misguided identification with sattva. My teacher is better than yours; my meditation practice leads directly to enlightenment; or even that knowledge is only in your head but you need to be in your heart - a judgment often directed at Vedanta students.

As soon as judgment comes and you think you are "better" than the other just because you live in sattva more often, beware! The ego is sneaking in again.

Nevertheless, let's return to the true meaning of sattva. In Vedanta, we call sattva the "revealing power " because it reveals our true nature as non-dual, actionless Awareness. In the Bhagavad Gita Krishna defines a sattvic person as, "The one who sees inaction in action is truly wise." He or she knows that all actions are coming from silence and disappear into silence.

Sattva is still, unmoving, and points inwards. It is the platform for spiritual understanding as well. The mind needs to be in a sattvic state to absorb and actualize the teaching. A mind that is dull or overactive will not have the energy and focus to bring these teachings into reality.

The Three Buckets Teaching

Here is a nice example of how you can understand the effects of the three gunas.

Imagine there are three buckets of water and the sun shines on all three of them.

In one bucket, the water is dirty and muddied. The sun is not reflected, but rather absorbed in the dirty water (tamas).

In the another bucket there is a strong wind that creates waves and a rippled surface. The reflection of the sun's rays is difficult to see (rajas).

Only in the third bucket there is a clear reflection of the sunlight because the water is calm and clear (sattva).

Be aware that all these gunas arise in You and disappear in You. You, as Awareness, are beyond the gunas. They need You, Awareness, to appear. They don't exist apart from You, but You, contain them all.

The Assimilation of Experience in Connection with the Gunas

An experience is an unbroken series of inner and outer events and the reactions and responses to them. Every experience has a beginning, a middle and an end.

The reaction in animals is programmed and instinctive. Humans have the power to think about an experience, to study them, to extract knowledge from them, and to free themselves from their programming.

For spiritual growth to happen, we need constant proper assimilation of experience, just like we need to digest food rightly, otherwise we suffer. If we don't assimilate experiences correctly, we will "suffer." We will not be able to extract knowledge from what is happening and this will compromise the development of our subtle body (conscious mind).

Like an animal, a human infant unknowingly acts out its subconscious tendencies. Once the intellect develops, it assimilates values, discriminates experiences, and begins to evolve - creating its own identity. The longer the experience remains unassimilated, the more problems it causes. We can observe this fact in adults that had difficult family situations as children.

The intellect is in charge of interpreting experiences. If they confirm to the ego's desires, it brings positive feelings. If they are contrary to the ego's desires, negative feelings arise. How it interprets experience depends on knowledge or ignorance and the three factors beyond our control: rajas, tamas and sattva.

The whole teaching of Vedanta is only for the intellect, because the Self, You, is already free.

Rajas

A rajasic intellect is not concerned with the truth of experience, but only with how the experience relates to the fulfillment of the ego's desires. It is always a source of frustration because everything you gain, you will ultimately loose as well! An object gained causes attachment, an object lost produces grief - and that does not make you happy!

Rajas causes the ego continually to seek fulfillment in new experiences and repeats actions that will produce suffering, which will prevent learning from experiences. When a pleasurable experience ends, it creates disappointment. If the experience is mediocre, in a way it is better for you, because you don't want to repeat it! If it is an undesirable experience, you want it to finish fast.

"More-better-different" is the mantra for rajas, as my teacher James always says.

Rajas is an aggressive, extroverted force - and because of that - it is always accompanied by tiredness and insomnia. If tamas appears, you cannot accomplish the to-do list - and if it doesn't come at night, you cannot sleep. So you suffer both ways.

Assimilation of experience only takes place when the mind is alert and present. When Rajas dominates the subtle body, the innate wisdom of the Self is not available to help the intellect.

When you are rajasic, your mind is dealing with daily desires, so you are too busy to look at your issues. They remain in the background causing suffering. The actions you make with a rajasic mind will be overly optimistic and strongly influenced by your ego.

I have often observed that people who go to Tony Robbins or other motivational speaker events come out highly pumped up with over confidence (we can make it!). Only to fall flat on their face once reality hits them.

Consequently, if you don't deal with your unresolved experiences because your rajasic mind does not let you, subliminally they will drain your attention from what needs to be done in the moment.

Tamas

Tamas is a veiling power that inhibits the assimilation of experience. Under its influence, the subtle body seems quiet, but it's actually just dull and unmotivated. Efficient assimilation of experience requires mental clarity. When a torpid veil covers the subtle body, perception is distorted and assimilation is compromised. The intellect is dull, so it can't connect results of actions with thoughts. "Where? What? I don't know," are the typical responses from a tamasic mind.

Unlike rajas, it dislikes change and anything new. It rather revisits old negative situations where it was feeling helpless and powerless, with a sense of depression. I call it the "poor me syndrome."

Tamas somehow solves a problem by either denying it or - with the help of rajas - puts the blame on someone or something else. A very rajasic lifestyle that exhausts you, creates tamas.

Other negative factors are the neglecting of your duties to yourself or to others. This can be the neglect towards your own cleanliness, the neglect towards your closest friends, or even towards your children.

Sattva

There are no experiential qualifications for enlightenment, only the right guna balance. If the mind is predominantly sattvic, it can assimilate information carefully and understand that experiences are not permanent.

Rajas projects, tamas obscures, and sattva reveals things as they are.

When rajas dominates the mind, desires interpret experiences. When tamas dominates, fear interprets experiences (both obscuring the truth). When sattva dominates, truth interprets experience.

If our causal body is full of rajasic and tamasic tendencies, then it is very difficult for sattva to shine through.

If I want to know the Self as it is (and assimilate that "I am Awareness"), I should cultivate a sattvic mind and turn my attention inwards.

We better get the right guna balance in our subtle body.

Rajas is great for motivation. Tamas can ground ideas into reality. In sattva we can discriminate what is real (Satya) from what is apparently real (mithya), creating a peaceful mind.

How do these gunas bind us?

It appears that the gunas seem to bind and limit the Self – that is forever free and unconditioned – by producing habitual thoughts, feelings, and actions. Rajas binds by longing, cravings and attachment (these attachments are sometimes called love by rajasic personalities). Tamas binds by ignorance and its effects. It is sometimes interpreted as knowledge, but it is just lazy ways of interpreting information. Needless to say, both create suffering. But even sattva can bind through attachment to happiness and knowledge. For example, the "new age" is attached to beauty, goodness, and truth - regardless of the fact that existence is not always sweetness and light!

I think everybody can relate to this interpretation of our subconscious tendencies. Its understanding is crucial in order to live a happier more fulfilled life. Even if you don't want to go for enlightenment, or however you want to call it, this knowledge will help you to understand yourself better. Once I brought the understanding of gunas into my counselling practice, I could see immediate results and changes in people. Once you bring a level of stillness and mindfulness into your life, the appearance of the gunas is easy to recognize and navigate.

3

THE FIVE PILLARS

The irony of Vedanta is that even though you are already what you are looking for – whole and complete, uncreated, actionless, ordinary, non-dual Awareness – you still require sadhana (spiritual practice) to purify your mind to a point that it can assimilate this knowledge.

In this chapter, I want to start with daily reflections and practices that you can relate to and do. Let's start with an obvious one.

A Healthy Body

When you are in physical pain it is hard to think of anything else other than the pain. Any thoughts about liberation are wishful thinking.

To keep the body healthy is not that difficult today. There is a lot of hype these days in the west around health. Move your body daily in some form of activity. Hatha yoga is great, but not necessarily the best practice for everyone. There is so much more like swimming, cycling, running, and even gardening or other activities that stretch your body and tone your muscles.

Eat a variety of fresh foods, not too much and not too little. Don't be obsessed with food, you are much more than the food you put into your body! Obsession with food is creating a tight and judging mind. "Eat for living, don't live for eating." In Ayurveda they say, "food is medicine and medicine is food."

I stopped being a vegetarian after 25 years. I eat what my body wants me to eat, and I eat what friends offer me. That is similar to Theravada Buddhism where wandering monks will eat whatever is offered to them. It is mostly vegetarian food because I love the freshness and how it makes me feel. I include fish and sometimes chicken in my diet as well. I see no change in my mental state or my health, but a relaxation and freedom that comes through my food choices.

Ok, healthy food, get enough sleep, don't take drugs. That should be an easy choice, but not for everybody. In some circles it is claimed that drugs can open your mind, and sometimes it is called "medicine." I am not denying that it can give you glimpses into the causal body (subconscious mind), so what is the problem? There are many different substances/drugs and some can be quite damaging.

Firstly, every drug experience is just that, an experience. What is the nature of any experience? That it has a beginning, a middle, and an end. It cannot be repeated, as hard as you might try.

Remember that every experience creates a vasana (imprint in your subconscious mind) and many experiences of the same kind create a samskara (a much deeper groove in your subconscious mind). This will create a craving for more experiences of a similar kind. Every time the impressions will be different, and subsequently, over a short time they will create an addiction.

Addictions have their own momentum and this book cannot go into this area in detail. Very rarely drug experiences are analyzed. People stop in the experience itself, not trying to understand the underlying knowledge that supports these experiences. So therefore you cannot receive the wisdom that might be revealed to you.

If you suffer from any psychological problems like depression or bipolar disorder, don't start that trip! There is a very good chance that your symptoms might reappear, as this happened to a very good friend mine.

There is a "filter" that protects the subtle body from the causal body (subconscious mind) and it should remain like that, otherwise we would not be able to function in the world.

And, last but not least, if you have a burning desire for truth (one of the qualifications in Vedanta that we will discuss in the next chapter) you need all your energy and focus in discriminating between what is real (Satya) and what is fantasy (or apparently real), mithya. You don't need to get lost in visualizations and crazy wild thought patterns.

So keep a healthy body and mind!

Live An Ethical Life

What are ethics? They are behaviors that are in accordance with dharma - the natural law of existence.

I heard the Dalai Lama (yes, sorry, such an old line) saying, "Live a good and just life." We know deep in our hearts what is "right " and what is "wrong," even though we don't always follow these intuitive feelings. A thief locks up his loot in the night, because he knows that taking what is not yours will have consequences. All spiritual traditions have some moral and ethical guidelines or rules. Some of these rules were established when the tribes were still roaming the deserts of the Middle East, and they are not applicable for us in the 21st Century. For example, not eating pork, having many wives, circumcision, etc. We have to separate them from realities in our century.

Some examples of these moral codes are the yamas and niyamas that Patanjali wrote in the Yoga Sutras; or the Buddha in the Noble Eightfold Path; or the 10 commandments in the Bible. They hint at the eternal laws that should not be overstepped if you want to live a quiet and fulfilled life.

To put it even more simply: you want a quiet mind. A mind that is in your control and not the other way around. A mind that is purified enough to comprehend the more subtle truths for liberation. A mind that is able to assimilate experiences as they happen and put them to rest. For this, a life that is supported by ethics is necessary.

Remember that every action leaves an imprint in your subconscious mind. In other words, it creates karma. Karma means action - and every action will create a reaction, like every cause will have an effect. This is not just a spiritual law, but a physical law as well.

It matters what you do and you can't get away with anything!

For example, imagine that you take what was not given freely. Somebody asks you about the object you took and you have to lie about it (another break of a universal law). Internally you feel bad about this (guilt) and you are on alert not to meet that person again (fear), in order not to be forced to lie again! (Deepening the vasana into a samskara).

When I was a poor student (aren't all students poor?) I tried to save money wherever I could, and I travelled on the public transport without paying the fare. I pretended to have a ticket (fear) and I was standing close to the exit doors to have a head start if/when the conductor was coming in. I was tense during the whole journey and it was only when I jumped out of the train that I felt a bit of joy in saving a few pennies. One day

I realized that if I pay the ticket price, I could relax, find a seat, read, and arrive relaxed at my destination. Needless to say, from that day on I paid the full fare and I was happy and relaxed sitting in the train, studying, and enjoying the view from the window.

Keep it simple! Don't complicate your life. In the end, you have to pay for your actions no matter what.

Life is a zero sum game! For every gain there is a loss. What does that mean? You cannot win in this apparent reality. For every up, there is a down. So you better follow the universal laws to stay safe and content.

And the highest universal law - drum roll please - is ahimsa: non-harming yourself and others. "Do unto others as you would have them do unto you," to quote the Bible. Or to put it simply, "Treat others as you would like to be treated."

Sounds simple like all the difficult truths, but is it? Unless there is a solid understanding that there is no other, it will always be a struggle for you, but a struggle worth having.

Karma Yoga

"It is better to perform one's own karma imperfectly than to master the karma of another. By fulfilling the obligations he/she is born with, a person never comes to grief." (Bhagavad Gita)

If you are visiting or living in an ashram, you might be familiar with the concept of karma yoga in the form of working in the ashram in simple jobs for a few hours a day. This is not karma yoga, but just free labour to maintain the ashram. There is nothing wrong with this if your attitude is that of serving and contributing.

However, karma yoga is actually one of the main purifying practices that every student has to undergo in their spiritual journey. It is the understanding that the outcome of any action is not under your control. Results will be facilitated in the dharma field in an impersonal way. If it suits the whole it will happen. If not, not. (Even if books like "The Secret" or other "positive teachings" disagree.) Your wishes have to be in tune with the needs of the total. Sometimes it happens that you get what you want, and sometimes it doesn't.

Understand this:

You (your ego) are not in control.

Something else is. And yes, you are not separate from that, even though it looks like you are!

Oh, Vedanta seems mad sometimes!

Karma yoga purifies you. It makes you humble and it gives you an appreciation and reverence for existence.

What do we mean by existence?

There are many words that have been used to explain it, but it is actually very simple:

That which is this apparent reality with all its rules and laws as it is observed by me, the Self.

Isn't it logical that the outcome of any action is not in your control? Think about it. Let's say you just finished a yoga teacher training and you want to teach your first class. You made a session plan, you hired a place, you advertised. In other words, you are ready!

The next morning it starts raining, can you do anything about that? Your car does not start and you arrive late. Only three students turn up because of the weather, and no one has done any yoga before. Is this your fault? Are you responsible for the low attendance? Can you blame the students?

No, the only "control" you have in mithya is the type of action you do, but not the outcome. Too many factors have to be aligned for it to work out the way you want it. Sometimes it does, sometimes it doesn't. Even though this might sound depressing for a controller or doer, think about considering the relief it can give you!

Anxiety is precisely this, worrying about an outcome you have no control over. Did everything turn out exactly the way you thought it would? Most of the time your fears are baseless.

Karma yoga humbles your ego. Knowing that you have no control, your ego cannot claim any special credit. Existence holds all the strings and you happily surrender to that. This surrender purifies your likes and dislikes as well, and in that process your vasanas get neutralized too. Karma yoga also balances your gunas. Rajas and tamas loose grip on you if you can relax your anxiety about the outcome of your actions. Your life becomes more sattvic and simple.

Meditation

In the Vigyan Bhairava Tantra there are 112 meditation methods and concentration techniques listed. Only very few mention the most popular in the west: the breath. There are many visualizations and other strange meditations. For example, sneezing. When you feel the urge to sneeze, wait and become very focused on the tingling sensations in your nose. It will get stronger and stronger, you stay alert without the impulse of exploding, totally focused, and then if you are skilled, the energy that would have been exerted with a sneeze will implode within yourself. There is a moment of no thought. In these scriptures it is written, "and then...and then..." without giving us a clear idea of what will happen. I don't know of anybody who "became enlightened" through this meditation practice, but who knows?

The point is that there are many practices and you have to find out what suits you. Let's reflect for a moment on the practice of meditation and why and how you want to do this.

If you ever walked past a new age bookshop in the last 20 years you will have read titles like "Be Here Now," or the "Eternal Now," or " The Power of Now," and so on.

If I tell you the past is gone and future is not here yet, you will not be surprised. The future in fact is only the past repacked and projected into the imagined future. Depending on your subconscious mind (or your vasanas and gunas), you will either project a positive or a more negative outcome. Both are only real in your imagination.

So what is left? The "now" you might say, in agreement with Eckhart Tolle.

The now is not a good word because it indicates that there is something like the now. But is it?

Show me this now, where is it? How long is it?

If I clap my hands, where is the now?

Even a clap has a beginning, a middle, and an end. So it happens in time and space. Where is the now, tell me?

The fact is you are always in the present moment, never somewhere else. This refers to the popular notion that you have to be more in the present. You cannot be more or less present. Yes, you might be present to your fantasies, but you are always present. Why? Because you are this non-dual, actionless, uncreated, unbound, ordinary Awareness.

So let's look into the present moment and discover what is happening.

All your senses will give you some input and your mind will decide what to focus on. The nose will perceive smells, the eyes will perceive sights, the body will perceive sensations, your tongue will perceive taste, and the ears will perceive sounds. Only through your senses you will be able to connect with the apparent reality around you, while your vasanas and gunas will project your likes and dislikes into this field.

So again, what is the now?

Perhaps a light breeze on your skin, the smell of coffee, a slight tension in your legs. All this is happening in the now.

The world is perceived by your senses and analyzed by your mind. To be present is really not such a big deal. Easy, but difficult at the same time.

This is where meditation comes in. We need to differentiate between:

a. Concentration as the unwavering focus of attention on a single object in consciousness (dharana).

b. Meditation as the effortless flow of sustained concentration (dhyana).

Patanjali clearly points out that meditation is not just sitting and relaxing. In fact, it is an "unwavering focus of attention." It takes effort or "tapas," as he would say. Only after the effort of concentration, meditation becomes effortless.

In Vedanta, the "single object" of concentration is the Self.

Who is meditating? Who is this me? Who am I?

Once you "get a sense of it," you can drop into it. When you can "stay" in the Self as the Self, it becomes effortless. It is only an effort in the beginning.

Why? Because of our old habits. We think we are our sense perceptions and we identify with the doer (the ego).

Meditation is not just sitting in silence and waiting patiently for the sky to open and reveal its secrets. Trust me, I was a great "sitter" when I was involved in Theravada Buddhism and later in Zen Buddhism. I could sit for an hour, no problem. My fellow meditators thought 60 minutes was for "beginners," so we sat for 90 minutes. When I sat with "Baba," a very relaxed and friendly Indian guru. He used to sit with us sometimes for two-and-a-half hours. After that, I felt great, spaced, sensitive, and high. Until I fell back again into my "normal" neurotic state.

Silence is not against ignorance. Baba was very extreme. In all the years I was with him, I never heard him talk about the scriptures, or even basic spirituality. His message was "enjoy yourself!" Not bad, but not enough for most seekers.

It is great to slow your mind down for a while, but remember, without an input it remains as it is. Unless you can assimilate the knowledge of your essence in a receptive mind, you will stay the same. Maybe a bit quieter and nicer, but not wiser.

"Meditation is an action not a means of knowledge." (James Swartz)

Knowledge/Teacher

Ok. You live an ethical life, eat healthy, meditate regularly, and develop some appreciation and reverence towards life - isn't that enough? The simple answer is no.

It is a bit like planning to go to a waterfall in a national park. You have great walking boots, some food and water, and a willingness to go. But no map. You only heard and read in some books that there might be a waterfall somewhere in this huge national park, but you have no idea how to get there. Because of your willingness, you start the trip full of energy and hope and ask the first person you meet, "Where should I go?" The first wanderer points in the left direction and you walk on, but the next person you meet points back to where you came from. You become confused. And the final straw might be somebody who tells you that there is actually nowhere to go. "The waterfall is within you."

The spiritual path for a beginner is a bit like that. All the Youtube videos, or seminars, or wandering gurus can confuse you even more. If you don't have a road map or knowledge about where you want to go, to get there takes a long, long time. And more often than not, one lifetime will not be enough.

Knowledge about where you want to end up and a teacher who embodies the direction you want to take are, for most of us, necessary. So where to begin?

It took me nearly 30 years to realize who I was, and to find the path that led me here, Advaita Vedanta. Why did it take me so long? You can only absorb a teaching when your mind is at a certain level of comprehension. That's why there are so many paths and they all fit somehow into the big picture.

In the introduction of this book I already mentioned my spiritual journey, but I want to explain it in more detail here.

I started with a very charismatic teacher, Osho, who fitted my idea of spirituality at that time. There was dance and meditation, sex, therapy and human interactions that suited me. I was ready for that level of transcendence, that was sometimes blissful and sometimes heart breaking. I was young and this was just the right entry into this new world.

I learned not to be ashamed, to have fun, to show my feelings and to be authentic in my interactions with others. On top of it, I learned a lot about male -female relationships and I got a good understanding about different spiritual paths and meditation techniques.

I had a great time, a bit like play school or kindergarten, a helpful preparation for the journey I was meant to travel later on.

So Osho was my first teacher during these 12 years. To break my attachment to this teacher, he had to die in order for me to continue my journey.

My spiritual path then led me to Buddhism.

After many intense Theravada Vipassana retreats, I wanted something even more intense (see how the mind works!).

So I followed a Japanese Zen teacher, who came to Australia frequently to do retreats. It had a different flavor (the mind loves new experiences). The structure was the same, if not more intense.

The idea was that if you sit long enough, knowledge would come to you in the silence of your mind. They never told us where that knowledge was hiding, but needless to say, for me it never showed its head. Yes, I got blissful feelings, insights and a more relaxed attitude towards life.

I lived a happy life with my wife and my two children, but I knew that my journey was not over. I wanted Moksha, freedom from limitations.

And after every experience, as blissful as they were, I had to come back to my unchanged reality.

After a while I felt like a hamster in the spiritual hamster wheel. I would sit longer, do more retreats, be closer to the teacher, read more books and then "I would get it".

The final straw was when I entered sarvalkalpha samadhi, a blissful state that lasted nearly three months. I thought I "knew" everything that needs to be known for liberation, but it disappeared slowly in the background. It left me confused … what to do now?

If I would have had more guidance during or after my samadhi experience, I would have avoided the "dark night of the soul" that followed afterwards. I felt utterly alone and spit out by existence itself.

I tried to turn my back towards spirituality. I stopped meditating and practicing other forms of spiritual practices that prepare my mind for insights.

I was briefly convinced by Neo Vedanta teachers that there is nothing you need to do , just be yourself and enlightenment will happen one fine day.

Everything that you deeply know will not be lost, as the Bhagavad Gita claims: "On this path effort never goes to waste, and there is no failure."One day I stumbled into my teacher, not knowing at first that this would be my last stop on this "spiritual trip".

I persuaded a friend to join me on a trip to Tiruvannamalai, a holy pilgrimage town in South India , situated at the foot hill of Arunachala, the sacred Shiva mountain. I went as a tourist, because I wanted to visit the Ashram of Ramana Maharishi (30 December 1879-14 April 1950).

I had a lifelong fascination with this sage. He had no spiritual preparation in his life and, when he was 17 years old, he felt that he was dying. Without fear he decided that if he was going to die, then he might as well help it along. He laid down on the floor and pretended to be dead. To his surprise, his body did not die but his intellect realized his true nature.

He went to a sacred mountain, Arunachala, to sit in a cave to meditate. After some time, disciples sat with him and, sixteen years later, living in two different caves, an Ashram was built around the bury ground (Samadhi) of his mother. He lived there until his death and he never left his beloved sacred mountain. This Ashram still attracts many devotes even today.

I was sitting in a German Bakery, a place where all travelers meet, in the sacred city of Tiruvannamalai. I spotted a friend and she waved me over to join a group and listen.

We were around five people listening to an elderly American guy (he called himself "a red neck from Montana") having a coffee and a cake. There was nothing greatly spiritual in the setting, apart from being in India.

His name was James Swartz, he looked a bit scruffy and little did I know that this meeting would change my spiritual direction for good.

The setting was so ordinary that I thought I would waste my time. It certainly was not a "love at first sight," but when I heard what he was talking about, my heart sang!

I found my teaching and I found my teacher!

This was what I was looking for, the pure logical knowledge of Vedanta.

James became a wise looking saint after his wedding with Sundari, who also became my teacher. I still have to smile about our initial meeting so many years ago.

I only write about my story to explain that a teacher is necessary, especially if your longing gets more intense and your understanding deepens.

Every journey will be different, therefore mine is in no way special. You will have your own milestones, your disappointments and your despairs, but be sure that if your mind is prepared, a teacher will come into your life.

You don't have to look for one, let the teacher find you.

The teacher will be in accordance with your understanding. There are no bad teachers, only teachers and lessons that need to be learned by you in that particular moment.

James made it very clear that he is just a vehicle for the teaching of Advaita Vedanta. In his own words he is, like all jivas (individuals), not perfect, but the knowledge of Vedanta is.

To understand this counter intuitive teaching, your mind needs to be qualified (more on this topic in the next chapter) and you need a teacher.

4

QUALIFICATION

The following qualifications were written by Adi Shankaracharya in the 15th century in his book, Vivekachudamani. He was one of the great reformists of Vedanta, and all of the modern Vedanta teachers express gratitude to him. He founded four large learning centers in the four corners of India that produce brilliant teachers to this day.

Before I list Shankaracharya's qualifications, we must address two very important concepts:

1) You can not find joy in objects.

Perhaps this sounds obvious to you but what motivates people in the west (and more and more in the east) as well?

To have more objects!

There is a true story about two rich kids in Australia who made a bet on who will have the biggest amount of toys before they die. The winner was declared a few years ago, when one had to go to prison for fraud.

You may argue that it makes you happy to buy a new car, or a new handbag, or some other object. True, it seems that happiness arises when a new desired object appears. But let's look at it closer.

If happiness is really in the object, then whoever has that object will miraculously feel happy. Sorry, the Prada handbag you so desire and are happy to buy leaves me unemotional.

So where is the happiness that you feel?

The answer should be clear by now, it is in you.

Once the object is acquired, the desire for it will disappear for a moment. The joy and happiness that you are and always have been will be recognized by you, like clouds dissolving to reveal the shining blue sky that has always been there. However, it will be clouded once again by a desire for another object, along with the fear of losing it or keeping it.

How long will it be till the next set of clouds cover your happiness again? It might take days or months, yet the joy will leave you again as soon as another desire overshadows it.

Not only material things are objects. Everything that arises in Awareness (You) is an object. This includes feelings and thoughts. None of them can give you permanent happiness, because of the simple fact that they don't last.

Knowing this prepares you for the second very important concept before we go into the main qualifications.

2) "Life is a zero-sum game." (James Swartz)

This means that for every upside there is a downside. You can never only win because there is always a shadow following every gain.

For example, you want money. When you have money you worry what to do with it because you don't want to lose it. You want a relationship. You found somebody, only to desire later to be alone again. The list goes on and on.

We live in duality, so you better get used to it. Accepting that you cannot win in this dualistic apparent reality, you accept every outcome as God's will or the will of Existence.

These are the qualifications according to Adi Shankaracharya:

Discrimination (Viveka)

A friend pointed out that the word discrimination is a fairly loaded term in our time. Please note that we are not referring to a discrimination of people from different backgrounds, religions, or sexes. We are referring to the discrimination of what is ultimately and permanently real, Satya, and what is only apparently real and changing, mithya.

We start with probably the most important qualification, because if you do know the difference between Satya and mithya, you are already free.

What is the definition of permanently real?

Remember, in Vedanta, real is that which never changes. What does never change?

Reflect on this. Everything changes constantly: your body, your feelings, and your thoughts. Nothing stays the same, except Awareness (You) that was/is shining on all these objects (your body, your feelings, and your thoughts).

In Vedanta we use Awareness and Consciousness interchangeably. I prefer to use the word Awareness because it is less polluted by interpretations and points nicely into something that you are aware of.

"If you can observe in life the stillness in movement and movement in stillness, you are truly wise," as the Bhagavad

Gita says. This implies that the stillness is you (Awareness). The movement, always changing, exists because you are aware of it.

Dispassion (Vairagya)

I had some difficulty with this qualification because I feel a lot of passion and intensity within me. Would that not be a great quality, to be passionate about moksha (freedom)?

Yes, that is actually the number one passion you should have. To quote the Bhagavad Gita again, "I am the desire that is not opposed to Dharma."

This dispassion refers to mithya, the apparent reality that is always changing. This neutralizes our likes and dislikes. If we become dispassionate about objects in mithya, we can put our hearts and minds into something that is in line with our dharma. We do our best and make an effort, but if the outcome is not what we wanted (we hit a brick wall or situations change), we can happily drop it, and just let it go. It is like a child that can drop a toy happily, even if he or she fought over it with another child.

When I was in India I saw Tibetan monks creating a colorful mandala on the ground of their temple. This went on for a month before it was finished, corresponding with completion of a month-long ritual. The ritual then concluded and the monks proceeded to destroy the mandala in one long stroke. No second thoughts, no hankering for permanency.

One example in my own life was when I started an intentional community with friends. We had the same vision of living sustainably while sharing resources and building lasting friendships. We planted thousands of trees in what was then a neglected cow paddock. We built roads and building blocks with electricity and water for 12 separate houses, and we also developed and implemented programs for community living.

Unfortunately, the people who joined us had different ideas about the future of the place and voted us, the founders, out of the important decisions the community was taking. Yes, I was passionate about the community, but my wife and I were able to leave it happily, after 12 years, without any regrets. No hard feelings, everything is constantly changing. That does not mean you don't get involved life, it means you become more dispassionate.

Six Disciplines for the Mind

1. Calmness of the Mind.

This qualification means that you understand that the mind is not under your control.

Can you tell me what thoughts your mind will come up with? No, you cannot.

What determines the content of your thoughts?

Your subconscious mind: your vasanas (subconscious tendencies) in combination with your gunas (qualities of the mind).

How to understand the contents of your mind?

At this stage, therapy can be very helpful to understand your repeating thought patterns. Of course, thoughts are not You and they are neutral. We give them power through our likes and dislikes. It is like when you wear colored glasses. With pink glasses, all looks pink. With red, all looks red. Thoughts are very powerful!

If you are with a group of friends and they all start sharing their worst experience, the energy in the room will drop and everybody will feel like crying. The opposite is true as well, when everybody shares their most blissful moment, the room will fill with joy. Both mind states were created by you in the way you allowed these thoughts to arise.

When you understand the source of your thoughts (the mind is nothing other than thoughts), you will be able to control your reactions to thought patterns and neutralize them. One of the ways to do this is to counter act a negative thought with a positive one. Yes, it might feel "fake" in the beginning, but why do you believe a negative thought more than a positive one? Both are based in projections and they are changing all the time.

"I am that in which these thoughts appear." (James Swartz).

If your thoughts are a bit too difficult to master, try your senses.

2. Control of the Sense Organs

Your senses give you messages all the time. Only if you act on them, they will disturb you. Same goes for your thoughts, the impressions that your senses will give you (smelling, tasting, seeing, sensing and hearing) are just neutral recognitions until you start interpreting and acting on them. So be careful when you open your mouth! Once a word has passed your lips it has a life of its own.

Feelings and emotions that are not expressed will not create bad karma. For example, these days you can post your comments on social media. Once you respond to a post in an unkind way, it will have life of its own. Remember how Trump held the world in tension, every time he wrote something on Twitter.

The Buddha apparently said, "Before opening your mouth, reflect, is it true? Or is it necessary to share? Is it kind?" Reflecting on this will give you some control over your senses. It separates you for a split second from your unconscious expressions of unexamined feelings. In this way no harm will be done.

3. Detachment from worldly enjoyments

Stay with one thing at a time! In our busy societies we often brag about our ability to multitask and to be involved in many different things. Most people complain that their mind is so busy that they cannot find peace from the constant stream of incoming information. With this influx of various thoughts, how can you focus on the Self and discriminate?

For a person longing for freedom this is another important qualification. And it is a value issue as well, how to choose your priorities in life. What do you really want? When the thought comes to sex, for example, you have no problem in staying focused, but "staying focused" on the Self is more difficult.

How do you get single-pointed? By practicing any meditation technique that suits your temperament.

4. Contentment

Once you understand that life is unfolding not as you would like, but how Existence wants it to be, you start relaxing.

You are secure in the knowledge that, as the Self, you are already whole and complete and nothing can be added or taken away from you. Knowing this takes away the underlying anxiety that most of us carry, and life will have the flavour of contentment.

5. Spiritual Courage

Spiritual courage was once characterized as a "male temperament," and it reflected the spiritual chauvinism of that time. What it means here is to be able to endure the little upsets that life throws at us. Interactions in life are full of little annoyances, like people being unkind and cruel. When you get too upset about this, you are easily being thrown out of your center, an indication that you need to work on equanimity and acceptance. This only refers to things that you can do nothing about. This is not a formula to be passive and act like a victim. It means to "stand up" to challenges, but not to be discouraged by small upsets and not take everything personally.

6. Faith

Faith is another important qualification, and in Buddhism, one of the obstacles in meditation is lack of faith. If you don't have faith that meditation can bring results, you stop and then of course there will be no progress.

In Vedanta, faith means that you can trust that you are whole and complete, based on the knowledge of the scriptures. You can have faith that there is nothing "wrong" with you because the scriptures tell you so. The scriptures tell you who you really are, unchanging Awareness. Have faith in that.

This knowledge is only for your intellect (buddhi) to understand. If you remain ignorant of this fact you will not realize your true nature, which will change your relationship with reality in many ways.

Vedanta is not asking you to have "blind" faith, rather it asks you to investigate with faith, the knowledge that the scriptures present.

Burning Desire for Freedom (Mumukshutva)

Without a burning desire for freedom you will not have the stamina to reflect on the teachings 24/7. The Buddhists refer to this longing as if "your hair is on fire." If your hair is on fire nothing else matters, right?

To illustrate this, there is a story of a disciple asking Ramakrishna, a saint who lived around 100 years ago:

"Master, what is this burning desire for truth? How do I get it, what do I need to do?" Ramakrishna kept silent and walked to the Ganges that flowed in front of his temple. When they both took a dip in the holy water, he held the head of the disciple under water. He struggled and fought hard, until Ramakrishna let go of his grip and he could come up and get some air. "Are you crazy?!" he screamed. Ramakrishna smiled and said, "What was your thought when you were underwater?"

"I only thought about getting air!" the disciple exclaimed. Ramakrishna said, "That is a burning desire, and just like that you have to think about moksha. Your whole life has to be dedicated to that, and you should not rest till you are free."

I live on a beautiful island in Thailand that is full of young healthy adventurous people who love to do yoga, dance around the fire, go to many workshops where "their hearts will be open," and the most popular workshops are the ones dealing with relationships and sex. Here on the island it is mostly called tantra, in all its modern new age western variations.

When I talk about Vedanta, the room is full of students who are keen to listen. If the next day offers another tantric shamanic sexual ritual, all the Vedanta knowledge is forgotten and finding a partner becomes a more "burning" concern. This is to be expected in young people, but with older people there are different obstacles.

Here on the island, people have time and leisure and it is mostly a holiday vibe. Back in what a lot of people call "the real world," there are other distractions like earning a living, taking care of children, and many more challenges that prevent them from living a sattvic life where a "burning desire " can be manifested. That's why the next qualification is necessary, and needed to keep you on track.

A Qualified Teacher

What is often not realized in this quest is that you, as a student, need to be qualified to find the teacher that suits you as well. In other words, you get the teacher you are ready to understand.

Conclusions about the qualifications:

This is a subject not many spiritual seekers want to embrace. Catering to that, many Neo Vedanta teachers are saying that you don't need any qualifications. That you are already free, so what or who needs to be qualified? It is a much better "sell" because all spiritual egos love to hear how advanced they are. Like a friend once said, "I am nearly enlightened," but she did not put any energy into the quest.

Measure yourself against these qualifications, but know as well that you don't need to be "perfect" in any of them. Just recognize honestly where you stand and work towards more clarity within yourself.

"Lord give me the courage to change what needs to be changed, the strength to accept what cannot be changed, and the wisdom to know the difference between the two." (Serenity Prayer)

5

MANDUKYA UPANISHAD

I often get asked that if there is only one reality without a second, what about dreams? What about the deep sleep state? What is real?

There is a great Upanishad called the Mandukya Upanishad, one of the shortest Upanishads, also known as "the king of the Upanishads." It explains that the whole cosmos is AUM, the universal sound or the universal vibration. AUM is made with no tongue movement, and is unique in any sound creation. According to the scriptures, it is the vibration that the whole universe is vibrating in, something modern scientist agree with. The word "amen" comes from AUM, and so it is not specific to yoga.

The symbol of Om, that you can find now on many t-shirts or tattooed on flesh, is not a letter in the Sanskrit alphabet, but the form that the vibration creates when it is uttered. I once witnessed how iron shavings on a plate shifted when the AUM sound was played. The shavings formed the Om symbol, and with slight variations in the sound, the pattern changed. This explains the difference in the Om sign from India, to Tibet, to Nepal.

Apart from the explanation that the whole universe is AUM, the Mandukya Upanishad explains the states of dreaming, waking, and the dreamless state (deep sleep). The three states of experience: waking, sleeping, and dreaming are the only way consciousness is manifested for a jiva (person).

The translation of Mandukya is "frog." So this frog scripture "jumps" around a bit. Who says that the old Vedantic teachers had no sense of humour?

Waking State

When we are awake our senses transfer pure perception of objects to our manas (mind), which is part of our subtle body and rules our emotions, feelings, and opinions. Our ahamkara (ego) is ready to be the doer (and hopefully, the enjoyer) of our actions.

The intellect (buddhi) will evaluate if this action is in accordance with its understanding or not. After, we act and this will create an imprint in our subconscious mind (vasana), in accordance to our values. So far so good, we think we are in charge and have control over our actions. We call this the waking state.

Dream State

In the dream state our senses turn inwards rather than outwards. Our evaluation will come from our subconscious mind, not from our conscious mind. A reversal of perception unfolds as dream objects arise. They are created by your storehouse of collected memories, and will be perceived and valued by your dream entity. This dream entity is totally controlled by subconscious imprints (vasanas). Yes, Awareness is still shining on objects, but the objects appear in your dream reality.

Have you ever wondered if what you are experiencing right now is not a dream?

You might read this and then wake up with the memory of reading about Vedanta. Why do you think what you see, feel, touch, smell, and taste now - is the reality?

Deep Sleep State

Let's analyze our deep sleep. It is the seed state, where vasanas are sitting dormant. You wake up from a deep sleep state and proclaim, "I slept so well! " If you, as Awareness, would not have been there, how can you tell? There has to be "someone or something" that was aware of that absence.

Yes, that is true. In deep sleep state, we are aware of no objects arising. Awareness is like light that shines with no objects that can reflect its existence. Therefore, the difference between the deep sleep state and the dream state is that, in the first one, all the internal senses are dormant and you only rest in formless consciousness. That's why it is so necessary for your mental health and refreshing for your body to be in this state.

Location of Objects

Let's look at the location of objects. And remember, I am not asking you to believe, we are simply examining our unexamined logic.

If I hold up a cup of tea and ask you where do you see this, you would say "I see you holding a cup over there."

Is that true?

First, you are actually seeing light reflecting on an object. Without light you would not see anything. Your eyes pick up a form that is brought through your retina to your mind. How close are you to your mind? A meter? A centimeter? Maybe a millimeter?

Of course not, you are the mind, meaning that Awareness is reflected in your mind and it is apparently You.

So I ask you again, " Where do you see this cup? " Yes, you see this, as you see the whole world, in You.

The world is in You.

In the waking state your intellect can function freely and question itself and the objects that are appearing in your mind. However, in the dream state that is not possible. In the dream state, the intellect's ability to reflect and analyze is diminished because the information it gets is not from external objects, but from internal vasanas, the imprints in your subconscious mind. This is why it seems totally logical that you can fly through windows or meet relatives or other loved ones who died long ago.

Can We Learn from Dreams?

I worked for many years in Australia in a Jungian psychology center and used dream analysis. As a professional, I could tap into the subconscious mind of my clients through dreams and discover many hidden aspects of their personality.

We can learn from our dreams. Of course, keeping in mind that whatever you experience and see in a dream is actually You. So your dead grandmother was created by some vasanas. It is not that she virtually appears and looks after you. She represents a quality that you associate with your grandmother, maybe kindness or generosity.

Even objects like cars, trains or planes are You in a dream. In a car, you, as a driver, are in control. In a train, you have to sit and trust the driver. In a plane, you have to surrender, as air travel is associated with lots of control issues and fears. Each one of those transport options represent an aspect of you.

Understanding this, you can use dream analysis to dive deep into your subconscious, and you can examine and neutralize your vasanas. Every dream is full of symbols that tell a lot about your subconscious fears and hopes that you are holding on to.

Janaka's Dream

Here is a very popular spiritual story called Janaka's Dream, which illustrates the topic of this chapter very well.

Raja (king) Janaka ruled over the country of Videha. He was once reclining on a sofa. It was the middle of the day in the hot month of June. He had a short nap for a few seconds. He dreamt that a rival king with a large army had invaded his country and slayed his soldiers and ministers. He was driven out of his palace barefooted and without any clothes covering him.

Janaka found himself roaming about in a jungle. He was thirsty and hungry. He reached a small town where he begged for food. No one paid any attention to him. He reached a place where some people were distributing food to the beggars.

Each beggar had an earthen bowl to receive rice water. Janaka had no bowl and so they turned him out to bring a bowl. He went in search of a vessel. He requested other beggars to lend him one, but no one would. At last Janaka found a broken piece of a bowl. Now he ran to the spot where rice water was distributed. All the foodstuff had already been distributed.

Janaka was very much tired of long travelling, feeling the hunger, thirst, and the heat of the summer. He stretched himself near a fireplace where foodstuff was cooked. Here someone took pity on Janaka. He gave him some rice water, which was found at the bottom of a vessel. Janaka took it with intense joy and just as he put it to his lips, two large bulls tumbled fighting over him. The bowl was broken to pieces. The King woke up with great fear.

Janaka was trembling violently. He was in a great dilemma as to which of his two states was real. All the time he was in dream, he never thought that it was an illusion. The misery of hunger and thirst and his other troubles were unreal.

The queen asked Janaka, "O Lord! What is the matter with you?" The only words Janaka spoke were, "Which is real, this or that?" From that time he left all of his work and became silent. He uttered nothing but the above words.

The ministers thought that Janaka was suffering from some disease. It was announced by them that anyone who cured the king will be richly rewarded, and those who fail to cure him will be made life prisoners. Great physicians and specialists began to pour in and tried their luck, but no one could answer the query of the king. Hundreds of Brahmins, well versed in the science of curing diseases, were put in the state prison.

Among the prisoners was also the father of the great sage, Ashtavakra. When Ashtavakra was a boy of only ten years of age, he was told by his mother that his father was a state prisoner because he failed to cure King Janaka. He went to see this king Janaka and asked him if he desired to hear the solution of his questions in a few words.

Ashtavakra whispered into the ear of Janaka, "Neither this nor that is real." King Janaka at once became joyful. His confusion was removed.

He joyfully explained, "The dream comes from me, is sustained by me, and resolves into me. Upon awakening from the dream I realized that the dream and everything in it, animate and inanimate, was only myself."

Janaka was already a highly esteemed spiritual seeker as we will see later in the Ashtavakra Gita (chapter 19), and that's why these "simple" words could free him of his confusion.

"Even as a great fish swims along the two banks of a river, first along the Eastern bank, and then the Western bank, in the same way the Spirit of man moves along beside his two dwellings: this waking world and the land of sleep and dreams." (From the Ramayana, an ancient Indian text.)

6

OBJECTS

We, as humans, have moved so far away from our identification with the Self that we project our reality outside, with the false belief that objects will make us happy.

All thoughts, feelings, things, places, people, and even relationships, are just objects appearing in Awareness. In fact, everything that is not the Self, is an object according to Vedanta.

For example, let's look at relationships, which can be confronting for some people:

We attach ourselves emotionally to another being, thinking that they will make us happy. This will end up in tears if we don't understand the reality of objects. Yes, in the beginning, they might make us happy and we are glowing in the attention we are receiving. However, what happens after the honeymoon is over?

The projection will come to a crushing halt and personality traits that were attractive in the beginning will transform. A strong personality can become a controlling partner. A sweet, loving person could become a needy, demanding partner.

If happiness was in the object, then, where is it now?

Can objects make you happy?

Yes, for a short time they can. You saved money for a new car and finally you had enough to buy your dream car. You are very excited. The car dealer is very nice to you. The interior of the new car smells very nice. The car shines and blinks, and you are ready to drive out of the dealership. This will be your most expensive drive. After that, you have a used car, but let's not spoil the fun.

You drive down the road. Hopefully you don't see the same car as a special offer advertised at the next car dealership. That would just spoil your joy right away. As you drive the car for a while, your excitement will be less. And then, one day, it is just another car you drive. Another better model will come around, and a new desire arises.

The examples are endless.

If the joy is in the object, the same object would give everybody the same joy. This is not the case.

So where is the joy coming from if it is not in the object?

The joy is your inborn nature, the joy is in fact, You.

Why do you project the happiness onto the object?

Because of the habitual nature of our senses to take us away from ourself, and not directing the attention to the inherent nature of ourselves: ananda/bliss).

Why do objects make us happy?

As we mentioned before, for a moment you don't have desires, and the happiness that you are comes forth. Objects are not only material objects, but every feeling and thought projected onto Awareness.

There is a lot of emphasis in following your feelings these days, but is this wise?

If feelings change, as they do, can you trust them? Furthermore, if you understand that feelings are created by your vasanas and the guna that is active at that moment, you should be careful following these feelings.

Thoughts are also another object illuminated by the Self. Thoughts, in themselves, do not imply knowledge. They imply knowledge only if the intellect is trained, disciplined, and is based in the understanding of your true reality.

Once I understood this, I had to surrender to the message of my teacher: "Don't trust your feelings or thoughts, they are all objects in the mind. Trust knowledge."

We don't want to chase experiences and objects. We want to be permanently content and fulfilled. A true spiritual seeker will not stop until he or she reaches this understanding.

7

THE KOSHAS

In the Taittiriya Upanishad there is a beautiful description of our nature and how we perceive it. It is called the analysis of the koshas, which can be loosely translated as the sheaths or layers that cover our human personality.

The five koshas are:

Annamaya Kosha

Annamaya kosha, the food sheath, is connected to your gross body. It is literally the body that is made out of the food we eat.

Are we our body? Most of us would identify with our bodies.

If we see ourselves as too fat or too skinny we apparently suffer. If we feel like we are not attractive enough, then our self- worth is affected. These days when we think our nose is too long or too short we might get it fixed. Or we suck fat out of our bodies only to realize after a while, that more and more things can be fixed, because we don't like ourselves.

Are we the body that we observe and judge? Does the hand see me or do I see my hand? The answer is clear, the body is an object that we can observe, so we can't be this meat tube that we are stuck in.

Pranamaya Kosha

Pranamaya kosha, the vital air sheath, is our subtle body, and is connected to the five vital airs and the five active organs.

The five vital airs are:

1. Prana: respiration and sensory perception.
2. Apana: elimination, reproduction, childbirth and, immunity.
3. Udana: thought, speech, exhalation, growth, and nervous system.
4. Samana: digestion and metabolism.
5. Vyana: circulation and movement.

What about our energy? We call it prana in yogic terms, chi in Chinese medicine, or ki in the Japanese language.

When we feel low in prana, is that you? When we feel strong and vibrant, are you strong and vibrant?

The blood that circulates in your body, the air that you breath and transform in your lungs, is that you?

The logic here is the same, the prana is just another object observed by you. It is changing all the time so it can't be you!

Manomaya Kosha

Manomaya kosha, the mind sheath, is also our subtle body, and is connected to the five cognitive organs and the mind (manas). This is our mind, our thoughts and our feelings. Identifying with this sheath conjures the saying: "Cogito ergo sum," a philosophical proposition by René Descartes translated as, "I think, therefore I am."

Thoughts and feelings arise and we easily identify ourselves with them. If it feels right, it must be right. But is it?

Feelings and thoughts change and they are run and dominated by the gunas, so you cannot be them. This is something to remember when strong feelings or emotions well up and you identify with the thoughts created by them. Don't trust them so easily!

But then what is left? We still have two more layers that apparently cover us.

Vignanamaya Kosha

Vignanamaya kosha, the intellect sheath, is also the subtle body and is connected to the five cognitive senses and the intellect. The intellect is that which learns and understands. That which selects information and draws the knowledge out of it. All knowledge has its seat in the intellect. Even the realization that you are whole and complete, non-dual, ordinary Awareness is for the intellect alone, because the Self is already that.

But are you the intellect, the knowledge?

No, knowledge can change, like everything in mithya. You are the unchanging witness.

Anandamaya Kosha

Anandamaya kosha, the bliss sheath, belongs to the causal body.

We all want bliss. The Taittiriya Upanishad describes this bliss differently to our typical understanding of it. It relates bliss to a state of deep sleep, which is Awareness without objects. In deep sleep we are not dead, but we are aware of no objects arising. The bliss that we are returns straight back to us. We feel great after a dreamless sleep with the realization that "I slept very deep and well." If no Awareness was there, who would know?

There is a samadhi state called nirvakalpha samadhi, where Awareness (You) shines on no objects. The problem in this Samadhi state is that your intellect is not involved, so you return to the waking state without a deeper transformation. We will discuss this topic in chapter fifteen.

This is not a "smiling, grinning bliss state." My teacher said that it would be better to call this state "ananta," rather than "anand." Ananta means fullness, ananda means bliss. When you are aware of your fullness and wholeness, where nothing can be added or taken away from you, you are content and happy.

This Taittiriya Upanishad stops here. Why? There is a reason for this and let's get into it with a classic story:

Ten monks went on a pilgrimage and they needed to cross a dangerous river. The leader wanted to ensure that all of them made it safely across.

Once they got out of the water, he lined them all up and started counting, "eight, nine..." One was missing! He started counting again and again, still one was missing. He panicked, "We lost a monk!" he screamed.

An old wise man heard his scream and came closer. This wise man heard his story and declared that he could find the tenth monk. "But how? " the monk shouted. "Relax," the wise man instructed, and ordered all the monks to line up.

As they did, he began counting them, "One, two, three, four, five, six, seven, eight, nine..." and he pointed to the leader, who was standing in line as well, "and ten!"

The leader realized his mistake. He forgot to include himself in the counting. How was this possible?

We do the same mistake. When we dismantle the five sheaths and wonder what is left?

You are left, you as Awareness.

If there is an experience of the five koshas, there must be an experiencer. Our mistake is that we are looking for an object when we are the subject, like the tenth person in the story. You are not an object of knowledge, You are the subject. Another way of looking at it is that in the field of knowledge, there is the known and the unknown. And then, there is the knower of both.

"You, as Consciousness [Awareness], are neither known or unknown, because You are the subject." (James Swartz)

In the Panchadasi, a brilliant Vedanta text, we have the example of sugar, milk, and water:

To make the water or milk sweet, you need to add sugar. Once you add sugar, it dissolves. In order to see something, you need to "add" Awareness, otherwise you can't see it. To see an object, you need to bring it in relationship to Awareness. This is another way of saying, you need to look at it! The essence of sugar is sweet, otherwise we can't call it sugar. The essence of Awareness is Awareness (Existence itself), nothing else needs to be added.

Imagine you see somebody in the distance in twilight. You only see the shape of the person, but you don't know if it is a women or a man, black or white, young or old. The only thing you know for sure is that this person is conscious. They would not be able to stand or walk otherwise.

What is the human body apart from flesh and bones, if Awareness does not pervade it?

Yes, just a meat tube.

8

SATYA AND MITHYA

What is unchanging and true for all of us? Something you can't deny about you and does not require any proof?

That you exist!

I heard a spiritual teacher saying that he doesn't exist, but who would say that? You exist because you are.

The other very important point you can't deny is that you know that you exist. You are aware of your existence.

In Vedanta, we call "this Awareness" Satya. Everything else is Mithya. Mithya is that which changes and Satya is the unchanging, unborn, limitless, ordinary Awareness that you are. Everything is in constant flux.

Buddhist philosophy is built on this fact: nothing is permanent and everything is changing continuously. This impermanence is being observed by the one factor that is permanent, not changing, also known as Awareness or Satya.

In the Bhagavad Gita, Krishna reassuringly tells us, "What is true (Satya) will always be true and what is changing (Mithya) don't worry about." This discernment is one of the qualifications to understand Vedanta (discrimination between the real and the unreal: viveka as discussed in chapter four). If you know what is always present and what is not, you are already highly evolved and just need a bit of a push to be ultimately free.

Mithya does not mean it does not exist. Because obviously for you it does exist. It is just not permanently real. It always changes, therefore you cannot make your happiness dependent on it.

Vedanta uses a nice example of a table and wood:

You see a table in front of you made of wood. There is no doubt that this is a table, but actually, if you examine it closely, you will recognize that it is just wood. Can there be a " table " without wood? Of course not. But can there be wood without a table? Yes. So is the table "real?" Or is it just a name and form made out of wood?

Would you say the table exists? Yes and no. It exists, but only because of the wood that made up the table.

In the same way, we say that our perception of reality exists, but it is not there without Awareness. What changes is born. You, as Awareness, are never born, so you are not affected by time and space.

Because your body does live in the world, it needs to be taken good care of. It cannot be discarded as unreal, or impure, or even sinful. The body is just a temporary container for the Self, where thoughts and emotions arise. Just don't be too concerned about all this impermanence.

Ramana Maharishi had cancer on his arm. He was being treated with every possible cure that Indians had in the 20th century. When they treated him, he just observed what was happening and let them do it. He had no concern about himself. He just said, "mud to mud," when they put another medicated wrap around his arm. I never forget a picture of Ramana on his last days, lying on the couch. His body was wasted and nearly dead, but his eyes were even more alive and the Self was shining through his body in the most powerful, radiant way.

Knowing what is just temporary makes life beautiful and relaxed. Everything changes! Moods come and go, bodies come and go, empires come and go, and even planets and solar systems come and go. What use is there to cling to anything?

The scriptures say that before the world was, Awareness was already there, and it will be there after this world is gone. So no need to worry. This sets us free to do whatever our dharma dictates (to discuss further in chapter twelve). We should do this with a mind that is free of the burden of success and failure. How can there be failure in something that always is and never ceases to exist?

Understand that the world does not need saving. We could do something to contribute to lessen the suffering of the world, because we act from a non-dual love, and not from the idea that the world needs fixing.

9

OUR BIGGEST IDENTIFICATION

As we mentioned earlier, our biggest identification in modern societies is with our own bodies. A fascination and nearly an addiction to how we look.

Since the arrival of smart phones, there is a compulsion in young people to take photos of themselves constantly (selfies). It indicates a very fragile sense of Self. One that is purely based on the apparent attractiveness of the body. After the picture is taken it will be uploaded to Facebook or some other social media, only to hopefully get flattering comments about one's physical appearance. Of course this apparent harmless "fun" act is creating a whole lot of new neurotic behaviors that deeply disturb younger and older people alike. Let's direct the wisdom of Vedanta on this phenomena.

It is such a deep identification, that I think we need to repeat the exercise:

Are you this body?

When I ask this in my seminars nobody stands up and says, "I am my body."

In Vedanta we state that who we are has to be unchanging in all three states: waking, sleeping, and dreaming (Mandukya Upanishad, chapter five). We can perceive the body, but the body cannot perceive us. The hand does not know me, but I can know my hand. The senses that are connected to the body perceive things outside and sometimes inside, but they cannot perceive me, the subject.

The body is a biological system. It dies, but the Self - me - never dies. Awareness never dies because it was never born. The body dissolves back into the five elements because it was created by them. The body is limited and is not constantly present. It disappears in both the dream state and in the deep sleep state. Even in deep meditation, in trances, dancing, or embracing a partner, the body limitations can dissolve.

Can you tell where you begin or end once you close your eyes?

In the third chapter of Patanjali's Yoga Sutras he talks about what can happen when we loose the boundaries of our bodies. We might get a sense of being big as the whole universe, or so small that we can sneak through keyholes. The body changes, but the Self (Awareness), never changes. There is no need to tell you that the body changes, it is clear. In fact, as you might know, we have almost a new body within seven years and a totally new cell replacement after twelve.

The Awareness of these changes never shifts. Awareness is always shining on different objects. The body has a shape. The Self has no shape. It is formless and it is everywhere. It is not confined to one particular place.

The body depends on its constituent parts and the five elements. What is the body without all the parts that form it? When is a body not a body anymore?

Am I a body without my hands? Yes. Without feet? Yes. Without heart? Yes. I can have somebody else's heart, but still call it "my body."

All these variable parts make up a body but I am, as the Self, partless and whole, independent of everything. There is a Japanese koan that explains this well, "Show me your original face, the face you had before your parents were born."

All these logical facts hopefully convince you that you are not your body. It should be clear by now.

Our next biggest identification is the identification with the mind.

Identification with the mind (Manas)

"You hurt me," " I am angry," or a very popular one used a lot in new age circles, "I need to protect myself from negative energy." Is this really true? Are you your feelings and emotions?

For the same reason you are not your body, you are also not your feelings and emotions.

Who is aware of them?

Yes, You as Awareness.

Like the body, feelings and emotions are not present in the three states of waking, dreaming, and deep sleep. They change all the time and are known by you, the Self.

Therefore can you be "hurt" by other people? Yes and no, a typical Vedanta answer.

If you are identified with your mind and body, other people can apparently hurt you. With a calm mind, you can observe old vasanas rising up. They can cloud your mind for a moment, but they will dissolve in the understanding of who you really are (Awareness).

Remember this "work" has to be done in the subtle body. This means cultivating a sattvic mind through meditation, training the intellect through knowledge, and neutralizing our egoistic tendencies through karma yoga.

Identification with the Intellect (Buddhi)

Are you the ideas you have about yourself?

Are you the thoughts or the identification with the role you play in this world?

For instance, a doctor or a lawyer, a husband or a wife, a spiritual person or a worldly person, a Christian or a Muslim. These are all just labels. However, for centuries people have fought wars about these identifications. Even now people are clashing because they belong to different soccer teams. Stupidity knows no bounds!

A quiet mind can easily observe that these labels are fabrications of a dualistic mind. It can rest in the non-dual nature of itself. In this lifetime you might change labels multiple times. For instance, careers may change, marital status might change, even our spiritual direction might change.

Awareness is the light that shines on all these labels. They dissolve in deep sleep or in a dream, and therefore they cannot ultimately be who you are.

Identification with the Ego (Ahamkara)

"I travelled to India," Really? Or did just your body go there?

"I went to a dance last night." Did you go there or did your "meat tube" go there and you claimed it was you?

This might sound stupid. But the ego is an idea you have about yourself, but it is not who you are. Egos are very unstable, as you know, so claiming it as your identity is full of danger.

A teacher once told me, "Don't make your home on a bridge, keep on going, your home is on the other side." What he meant by this was never settle with half-cooked ideas. Keep searching for the truth, until there is no more doubt in your mind. You have to leave all these identifications behind. Only then are you ready for the ultimate surprise!

You have "known" the Self all along, but it was so deeply hidden from sight that you discarded it as not important. Once you "understand" your true nature, even though it cannot be known by your mind, it cannot be forgotten. Like you never forget if you are a man or woman, or you never forget your name.

What is left? Often just laughter because you missed the most obvious thing in your life.

10

DOERSHIP

Are you the doer of your actions?

This may be difficult to understand. Let's start.

What do you know for sure? What is certain for you without any doubt?

Right, the fact that you exist. Along with this, you are aware that you exist. The understanding that you exist and that you know that you exist, is what the great yogis called sat. You are Sat Chit Anand. It comes from "Satya" (Truth of your existence) and "chit, " which is from "chidakash" (Consciousness). Sat and chit cannot be denied. Understanding this will bring fullness and wholeness (ananta) that will give you a sense of contentment and joy (ananda).

Check the triangle chart in chapter 20. Awareness is at the top of the triangle, followed by the causal body underneath, then the subtle body and finally, the gross body. Bear in mind that Advaita Vedanta claims that there is only one reality without a second.

You are Awareness. The Self is Satya and the three bodies are referred to as mithya, the apparent reality. Only the Self is eternally real. The three bodies are part of mithya and they come into play with every human life. The Self remains.

So, again, who is actually acting out?

Awareness, by its very nature, is not a doer, yet it is what makes all things possible. Like the light in a movie theatre, it does not do anything but still makes the picture appear. Or like the sun that shines and, by its light, makes everything come to life.

Remember this: according to Vedanta, an impulse is received by the sense organs to the mind (manas). The mind evaluates the impulse according to its likes and dislikes. After that it sends the information to the intellect (buddhi) and the intellect decides on an action, according to the gunas and vasanas (causal body). Only then the doer of action comes in, the ego (ahamkara), and acts.

You, as the Self (Awareness), are like the light shining on a white screen. You are not doing anything, but without your presence nothing would happen. Satya, the eternal Awareness, does not need mithya, the reflected Awareness. Mithya needs Awareness for its very existence and is not separate from Awareness. It comes out of Satya like a spider web comes out of the spider. The spider web needs the spider to exist, but the spider can exist without the spider web.

The fact is that You, as Awareness (Satya) don't act. By the light of Awareness, actions happen. Nothing actually happens to You, but by your own light, the whole world keeps on spinning. Isn't this amazing to realize?

It is a huge relief to be free of the burden of doership. You feel very relaxed. Not just because you don't have to act, but because you understand that you lack nothing and that you cannot lose anything.

A practice to help realizing this is karma yoga. It is especially for the ego, which is identified with the doer. It does not negate action, but it negates the idea of control over the results of actions. Negating this frees the mind of existential anxiety. We will discuss karma yoga in chapter 13.

The cause of existential suffering is the burden of doership.

11

DO WE HAVE FREE WILL?

This question is often asked in my talks. How much free will do we have to decide what we want to do?

When we think we have control over our actions, what are we referring to?

Do you have control over the growth of your body? Do you have control over any function of your body, like digestion, heartbeat, breathing, and so on? No.

Do you have control over your emotions arising and disappearing? Yes, once they appear you have some control of what you want to do with them. However, you have no control over them arising.

Let's analyze our thoughts. Do you know what you will be thinking in two minutes from now? Do you have any control over what thought will arise in your subtle body (mind)? No.

We can continue analyzing our activities during the day. You may think you have control over what you want to buy in a supermarket, or what you want to order in a restaurant, but you are not aware of all the marketing manipulations that are happening to your so-called "free choices." It is actually getting worse now. Every website you click on will leave a trace of your preferences. You are getting more and more manipulated by marketing strategists.

Even without all these subtle and not so subtle strategies, how "free" is your decision making from a Vedantic point of view?

The gunas and vasanas are the very forces that influence our decision making all the time.

For example, you wake up with a tamasic mind. You had the intention of going jogging in the morning. What will your motivation be? Most likely, you will turn off the alarm and keep on sleeping. After an even longer sleep, you wake up more tamasic. Your emotions will be based on self-doubt and a defeatist attitude: I can never do this, I am lazy, this will never work. You then proceed to dig into your bacon and egg (tamasic) breakfast.

If you wake up rajasic, you will jump out of bed and rush here and there. You may exercise more than necessary and look into the mirror after the work out, adoring your toned body and dreaming of who you will impress with this beautiful "you." The ego is in full power. No time for breakfast, you have a coffee (rajasic) on the go.

When you wake up rested and relaxed, in a sattvic mode, you do your spiritual practices, followed by some exercise, and then have a healthy breakfast. You are ready for the day!

To summarize: You have no control over your gunas, they arise and disappear.

Vasanas, as I stated earlier, are past impressions in your causal body. Every action leaves a "fragrance," an imprint depending on your likes and dislikes. They are known as "ragas" and "dveshas" in Sanskrit. The actions you like will leave a desire for more. The actions you don't like will leave a negative imprint, so you will try to avoid them.

Actually, the past is gone and every moment is fresh. Only our minds are stuck in past impressions, which influence our actions in this moment.

There are even more subtle imprints that influence us, like our karma (the residue of causes from the past that produces effects now: The Law of Cause and Effect). Another subtle imprint is our svadharma, which is our inborn nature. We will discuss this in the next chapter.

Considering all these factors, our "free will" looks shaky, doesn't it? Are we just robots then? No, otherwise no moksha can "happen." We can go against the current of unconscious desires and have one ultimate desire, to be free. Most of us do act and live as robots though.

When I worked as a counsellor, clients often said, "this behavior is just who I am, I cannot help it." It is easy to predict how their future will look. It takes an intense longing for truth to swim against the habitual stream of unconscious desires and behaviors. That's why mumukshutva (burning desire for liberation) is mentioned as one of the most important qualifications to understand Vedanta and the essence of who you really are.

So, do we have free will or not?

I conclude here with a statement one of my teachers said, "Act like you have free will, but know that you don't."

12

THE THREE DHARMAS

Dharma is a vast subject in Vedanta, and like everything in this book, I can only give a hint of what it represents.

There are three dharmas:

- Samanya dharma: refers to the universal values.
- Visesa dharma: the individual interpretation of the laws.
- Svadharma: the individual conditioning, your inborn nature.

Samanya Dharma

These are moral laws that govern the field of existence. They apply to everyone without exception and include non- injury, truthfulness, and so on. Samanya dharma is also the dharma of the macrocosmic level of physics, such as electricity, gravity, etc. They work on anybody regardless of race, gender, or situation. You cannot change them. You can only understand them. If you try to go against them, you will suffer their consequences.

Visesa Dharma

This refers to the process of how the individual interprets the universal laws and applies them to his or her individual reality. It includes everything: how they behave in a relationship, how they interact at work or with family, and in every other aspect of their lives. This will vary from person to person, and it will depend on their value system and their inborn nature. Sometimes you might have to use a white lie to support the moral law of non-violence, for example. Other times you might use a white lie to avoid hurting somebody's feelings.

Svadharma

This is your individual conditioning. It's the nature and predisposition with which every person is born. To be happy, each individual needs to act according to their inborn nature, otherwise, they will suffer. Because of the apparently unlimited choices, lots of people that I meet are struggling to find their svadharma.

Let's reflect for a moment on how most of us are raised. Following your school years (and sometimes already within that period), you are asked to make choices about what you want to study. You are also required to take courses you are uninterested in. You finish school at around age 17, which is when you have to make a decision about what you want to do for the rest of your life. What are you interested in at this age? If you are anything like me, it was to have fun with the opposite sex and explore the world. At that time, I had no idea what I wanted to do with the rest of my life. Who will make the decision for you? In most cases, your parents will do that for you, or maybe other outside people that "know you."

It usually depends on your exam grades and if there is a spot available in the program you want to enroll in. After you study, you discover that working is very different to what you anticipated. However, you struggle on for a while because you don't want to disappoint the people who supported you.

Something can happen later, known as "midlife crises." These days it happens much earlier and often around the end of your twenties.

What do I want to do with my life? What gives me joy, what motivates me?

There is a popular expression from Joseph Campbell, "follow your bliss," referring to the way we can investigate what makes us happy and find our fulfillment in life.

Reality is non-dual, but in mithya, in duality, we become apparently unique. There are infinite ways in which gunas, karma, and samskaras/vasanas interact, producing different expressions of human beings. All uniquely programmed to live this life and to (hopefully) realize the source from where they all emerged and will return to (Satya, the non-dual reality).

It should be easy to know your own individual program, yet it isn't.

Discover your Svadharma

How do we find our svadharma?

Through inner reflection, and not being held back by fear.

If there is a longing in your heart to express your creativity in a certain way, just do it! It does not mean that you quit your day job straight away, unless you have the means to do so. You can find ways to incorporate both. We only find out what our svadharma demands by doing it, not by fantasizing about it.

When you say yes to life, it will slowly emerge what Ishvara (Existence) has in store for you! If it is true that we are non-dual Awareness (the scriptures and our teachers tell us so), then through our intention and inner reflection, a path will open up for us!

Knowing that we are not separate waves in an ocean of consciousness, we allow and surrender to the will of the whole (Existence, God, the dharma field or whatever you think keeps the world spinning).

It often does not come in a straight line. Here is a personal story to illustrate this point:

I was teaching a seminar when a woman I have never met before approached me and asked me if I wanted to work with her. The job offer was as a change consultant in Melbourne, about 3000 kilometers away from where I was living with my family. I informed her that I had never worked as a change consultant and that, in fact, I was a therapist and a counselor. She insisted that I was just the man she was looking for.

I had already been contemplating changing my line of work because of a certain boredom. I was not sticking affirmations on my bathroom mirror or pinning wish lists to my fridge. Rather, I was patiently open to what might appear in my life. It was unclear if I was up to the task, but the woman insisted that I could do it. She would train me, so I just said yes, ok, let's do it.

It was by no means easy to first persuade my loving wife to move to a city with cold climate, and to take my son out of school and move house. We knew that this was a good opportunity, so we agreed to accept the offer. We found a beautiful house in Melbourne, my wife found some work, my son entered school, and I started working. Well, I realized early on that this might not be my svadharma.

I was not a bad consultant, however the work and the work ethics were not in harmony with my spiritual values. So after a year I said to my loving wife, "darling let's move on." She said yes, so we took my son out of school, put all our furniture into a storage shed, and decided to move to New Zealand.

I had many students and friends there. It turned out that my wife did not want to live so isolated in the country, so after two years we decided to go back where we started, to Byron Bay in Australia.

We ended up where we started, but the journey had changed us and we both knew that it was a great learning experience. Even though the constant change was challenging, the experiences we had on the way were very valuable and brought us to the next chapter in our journey.

Shortly after I returned, I started to practice yoga. Soon I began helping my yoga teacher to establish Byron Yoga Centre, which is now the biggest training school in Australia. I trained many students in yoga and meditation, and I could do what I loved the most, sharing my love for Advaita Vedanta. I had finally found what my heart was searching for: my svadharma.

So how do you know you have found your svadharma?

When what you do has a meaning for you. When it is not the money you receive that motivates you. When the amount of work is not a burden for you. When the creative process lifts you up. When even in the midst of chaos, your mind is focused on your goal. When even if the outcome is not as you expected, you take this as prasad (a gift from Existence). Of course, this is karma yoga in practice: you understand that you are not in charge of the outcomes of your actions.

It is rewarding to jump into the unknown, to learn valuable lessons from mistakes, following your heart and trusting in Existence. This could send you to another adventure that might be more aligned with your svadharma.

As my father used to tell me, "In great undertakings it is very valuable to have at least tried."

Take this to your heart: you have nothing to loose. Finding your svadharma is your birthright!

13

YOGA PATHS

Traditionally, there were two major yoga paths:

- Karma Yoga - the yoga of action.
- Jnana Yoga - the yoga of knowledge.

On the 11th of September in 1893 in front of the Parliament of World's Religions, an Indian monk known as Swami Vivekananda spoke. He explained the history of yoga and included bhakti (devotional) and raja yoga (control over the mind and emotions).

Let's be clear, these yoga paths will lead you to a destination. There can be rocky paths, slow paths, and direct paths - but they all should lead to the same goal, Self-knowledge.

Karma Yoga

Vedanta clearly states that all the karma paths, based on performing actions, are necessary "leading errors." This means that they are necessary preparations to understand the non-dual nature of the Self.

As we know, karma means action. The understanding is that we need to "do" something in order to attain an experience of bliss or a peaceful mind. Doing good deeds, of course, is not necessary. We are already whole and complete, non- dual, ordinary Awareness. If this is correct, and the scriptures tell us so, what we need is knowledge and not action, to understand our true nature.

The idea that we don't need to do anything, like the Neo-Advaita teachers are proclaiming, is very confusing as well.

We need both: action yoga (karma yoga) to purify the mind and knowledge yoga (jnana yoga), to understand our unchanging nature.

Under the umbrella of karma yoga there are many different yoga paths. Hatha yoga is one of them: you do asanas for inner strength and outer strength. Through connecting your breath with each movement (vinyasa), you can start slowing your mind down. Clearly, even if you have done a perfect asana (is this even possible?), it can only be a preparation for quieting the fluctuations of your mind (regardless of what Mr. Iyengar said).

Why is that? Because if you are already Awareness, there is nothing you can do to get it. You only need to train your intellect to understand it.

Bhakti Yoga

Bhakti Yoga is a great entry path for people who are emotional and passionate. Sometimes it is called the path of love. If your heart is melting with songs of the Beloved, you love to dissolve in ecstatic dance, and chant the name of the Lord - then this path is for you.

The realization should be that you are the love that you were looking for. This path is full of joy, laughter, longing, and inspiration. That's why we call it an entry path.

You need to understand the nature of love. If it is still entangled in dependency and a lack of self-worth, then some therapy might be necessary. In Vedanta, this love is understood as non-dual love. It is the love that is your true nature. It is not focused on another person, but it is the love of the Self to the Self, You.

Very rarely does bhakti yoga stand alone. Generally, it is connected with karma, raja and jnana Yoga. When you understand the non-dual nature of Existence, devotion will come effortlessly.

Raja Yoga

The scripture of raja yoga is Patanjali's Yoga Sutras. Raja translates from Sanskrit as king. It is considered the royal yoga path.

One of my Indian teachers told me that only kings would have the time to follow them. I am sure he did not mean this literally, but it is true that it requires a lot of discipline and time, in order to achieve a high level of concentration and meditation.

It disappoints me when I see young western students, who seriously want to study hatha yoga, being confronted with these highly technical texts. It really needs an experienced teacher to explain the Sutras, and it needs an even stronger commitment from the student to follow these techniques.

Once you can master these Sutras, you will be highly qualified to jump from the dualistic path of raja yoga (based on performing actions) to jnana yoga (based on knowledge).

Jnana Yoga

Jnana means knowledge. This is the yoga path this book is about: the yoga of knowledge.

Critics coming from other yoga paths often judge this path as being too intellectual, dry, and boring. We need to understand that you are also using the intellect for all of the other yoga paths. Only the intellect will hold and assimilate knowledge.

Within jnana yoga there are different approaches as well. There are dualistic schools and there is Advaita Vedanta, the path that is explained in this book. It is the most radical of the jnana yoga approaches, and therefore is very difficult to explain.

Jnana yoga states that there is only Awareness and nothing else (Advaita is translated as not two). There is only Awareness, and you are that! (In Sanskrit this statement translates to: Tat Tvam Asi.)

Jnana yoga varies from other paths in that it proclaims that there is nothing you can "do" to attain "that Awareness." It is not a state that changes with experiences and you are already it. If you are already what you are searching for, then what you need is knowledge to understand it. Vedanta will give you the knowledge that will clear up your doubts, as it is a "means of knowledge" (as the eyes are to see or the ears to hear). With its help, you will discover the unchanging truth of your own Existence.

Just to make it clear, Advaita Vedanta is not against other yoga paths. Most of us need to go through all the experimental paths in order to be ready to absorb this teaching. I explored the other yoga paths, and nearly all of my friends went through the same journey. The experimental paths are "leading errors" and necessary to be able to absorb Vedanta.

14

ETHICAL GUIDELINES

There is a common argument that without the Ten Commandments, we would still be savages roaming around and killing each other, with no regards for our fellow beings. Only organized religions gave us the framework to become civilized. But is this really true? I don't think so.

The Dalai Lama said his only religion is kindness, just being a "good person." Are we intrinsically "bad people" when we are left on our own? The answer is: no! Everybody knows deep in their hearts what the "right thing" to do is.

Here is a good example:

If there is a fire in a house being witnessed by strangers and somebody screams, "there still is a child inside!" immediately one of them might race into the burning house to rescue the child. When they are asked later why they risked their lives for this unknown child, their answer is often similar, "I am not a hero, I did what anyone would have done in my position."

There is an intrinsic moral compass in us that is based on the collective subconscious mind. That's what we usually forget and we follow our instinctive behavior, which is based in fear and desire.

Remember that Christians have the Ten Commandments and the Buddhists have the Eightfold Noble Path. Patanjali brought in the yamas and niyamas: moral guidelines to remind us to "do the right thing."

Before we examine these guidelines, it is important to be aware of what happens if we don't follow them. If we don't get caught, we think we don't suffer the consequences, but that's not true. Just like there are physical laws that we cannot negate (gravity, for example), we can't push spiritual laws away either, hoping they will not affect us. Yes, the fruits of our actions might come much later, or as the yogis believe, might even come during another lifetime. If there is a cause (action) there will be an effect (reaction) to everything we do.

The first "instant karma" we get when we do an adharmic action (an act that is not in harmony with dharma) is to feel bad about what we have done. We know it was not the right thing to do, but our mind gives us rationalizations that it was ok and that contradicts our "gut feeling."

When you value the truth and a quiet mind, you better "do the right thing." What is the right thing?

Follow dharma (read chapter 12 on dharma). The basic rule of dharma is: treat others like you want to be treated.

There are five yamas and five niyamas.

The Yamas (social observances)

In the second chapter of the Patanjali's Yoga Sutras, he explains the ashtanga yoga path. It is the ethical path Yogis should follow to achieve a focused and quiet mind.

1. Ahimsa: non-violence and non-harming in any form to any living creatures.

This supports compassionate living, as true non-violence is a state of mind and heart.

This is a deep subject:

How violent are you in self-talk?

How violent are you on a yoga mat or in the gym?

Do you need to be a vegetarian in order to be a good yogi?

What is non-violence in a relationship?

I can't get into all the subtle nuances here that this yama entails. Keep in mind the "golden rule:" reflect on how you want to be treated. Following this, you might find a direction to manifest ahimsa in your life.

2. Satya: truthfulness in mind, word, and action.

This is another complex subject. Nobody wants to be lied to. Sometimes we don't mind a "white lie" to keep us positive: "do I look good in this dress?"

Being truthful is being non-violent, and it will help us to have a quiet mind. If you tell a lie, it needs constant maintenance and this will make it very difficult to stay in a sattvic (peaceful) state of mind. This will deepen negative vasanas.

We use the word Satya to refer to "that which is real, that which never changes" in comparison to Mithya: "the apparently real, that which keeps changing".

3. Asteya: non-stealing, in order to free us from possessiveness and envy.

When you take what is not yours or freely given, you violate the first two yamas: ahimsa and satya. The result will be a disturbed mind. The whole aim of the yamas and niyamas is to create a quiet mind, one that is able to concentrate and to be still.

The need to take what is not freely given shows a lack of trust in Existence. If Existence wants you to have it, you will get it one day, if not, not. Relax and be happy with what you do have.

4. Brahmacharya: traditionally it meant abstinence from sexual interactions and the practice of moderation in all things.

This was absolutely clear: the celibacy required by all monks and nuns. However, when yoga came to the west, its meaning changed, but the underlying message is still the same. Deal with your sexual impulses wisely. Most of the great yoga schools that were established in the west have had some issues with this yama (Bikram Yoga, Anusara, Shivananda, and other schools all over the world).

Stay honest and have clear boundaries. A more modern version of Brahmacharya, adapted from Buddhism, is moderation: the middle path, as Buddha said. This means don't study or practice too much or too little, don't eat too much or too little, stay balanced in everything you do.

A mind that goes too much into extremes will be inflexible and not able to absorb the subtleties of the teaching.

5. Aparigraha: non-greed, in order to simplify life, and adopting an attitude of generosity and non-hoarding.

"Live simply so that others simply can live." Mahatma Gandhi's revered words sum up this yama.

Be mindful of the interconnectedness of all lives and treat your environment accordingly. One of the reasons why our world is in such a mess is because we have lost sight of the fact that we are One, and not separate from Existence.

Being generous, sharing our resources, and recycling what we can, makes us feel good and makes this world a better place.

The Niyamas (individual observances)

1. Saucha: purity and cleanliness of body, mind, and environment.

Be aware of what goes into your body because it will influence your gunas (energies) and consequently, your emotions.

Be aware of what goes into your mind. You can get exhausted through useless information and gossip that will cloud your intellect.

Be aware of your environment because your well-being depends on the well-being of the planet. Treat it as you treat your own body.

2. Santosha: cultivation of inner contentment, understanding that others are not responsible for our happiness.

"Shit happens" is an expression that we often hear. To put this into context: situations arise and you have no control over them, but it is up to you how to respond. Others are never responsible for your well-being. It is up to you to transform negative emotions into a state of equilibrium.

This can be accomplished through a whole lot of practical tools: meditation, psychotherapy, chanting, and even dancing.

However, Vedanta has the final tool: understanding through knowledge that you are Awareness, whole and complete, and nothing can be taken away from you.

3. Tapas: being able to control and confront your inner urges, mastering the direction of your efforts.

Without tapas - an inner fire and direction - no progress is possible, neither in life nor in spiritual pursuits. This inner fire and effort needs to be balanced with ahimsa (non-violence) so you don't go into extremes. I love the saying, "just do it!" This is the spirit of tapas.

When you know you don't want to do something, then don't do it. But never stay suspended too long in indecision.

Remember, energy never stands still, it either moves up to a feeling of well-being and happiness or it spirals down to final depression.

4. Svadhyaya: Self-study.

Not only study the scriptures, but also understand your inner motivations. Develop understanding of the Self.

Pattabhi Jois, the founder of ashtanga yoga, said, "just do it and all will come." He also said "Yoga is 99% practice and 1% theory." However, we know that a disturbed mind wants to do the same thing again and again, expecting different outcomes.

If there is no knowledge in what you are doing, no physical effort will help you to discover the underlying laws that motivate you.

Svadhyaya means never stop learning. This is the beauty and mystery of life as well.

5. Ishvara Pranidhana: devotion, dedication and surrender to the divine presence within all life.

Ishvara is another name for Existence, or if you prefer, God or the dharma field. Pranidhana means devotion or surrender.

Here, in the last niyama, Patanjali refers to the grace in Existence. After all the "work" is done with the right karma yoga attitude, there is nothing left but surrender and pray for grace. You are not the doer or enjoyer of the fruits of your efforts: Ishvara, God, or Existence is.

A heart that can feel gratitude and surrender is already full of joy. This will be the fertile ground for liberation to "happen."

15

MEDITATION AS A TOOL

My meditation journey started over 35 years ago. The techniques I used to practice involved a lot of huffing and puffing before I could sit quietly for 15 minutes.

The idea was that first the body needs to be exhausted before the mind can settle down. It was probably quite true for me back then. I was not able to sit quietly for any extended period of time because of my busy mind. However, after a few years of jumping and dancing and screaming my head off, it was clear that this was a very limited practice. I recognized that the screaming only gave temporary relief to my internal emotions. A few hours later they appeared again, ready to be released at the next day's meditation. This was no long-term solution and very much a beginner's meditation technique.

I loved the silent spaces that appeared a few times and I went deeper into them, discovering the Buddhist form of meditation known as Vipassana. In Vipassana you don't move your body and you have to sit motionless for extended period of time, watching the breath and sensations arising and disappearing. This cultivates a quieter mind, and also a very sore body.

I continued my exploration with meditation moving into zazen, which was "just sitting." Zazen is a very disciplined and intense form of mindfulness. As you can imagine, I became very good at sitting motionless for long periods of time, just observing my fluctuating mind. The idea was that suddenly a satori would happen, which is supposed to be an intense flash of insight. This would resolve my doubts and create clarity about the nature of my existence. Yes, insights came but they were not lasting, and soon the old habits of my mind returned.

What was I doing wrong? The answer my teachers gave me was that I should continue meditating and "all will be clear one day." It did not help that one of my expectations was that enlightenment would strike me as a flash of light, and I would walk around in a ball of bliss for the rest of my life.

Well, a flash of light did actually hit me after some long meditation practices, but it was more a curse than a help. This prolonged state of insight and bliss extended to nearly three months! After, as any experience, it disappeared. It happened so slowly that I only noticed it had dissolved fully after three months. A form of depression followed this process.

It felt like being kicked out of paradise. For these precious months I felt like I knew who I was, I understood the nature of Existence and the meaning of love. This experience faded and I forgot it again! Before that I had a certain identity as a seeker of truth, now that identity had collapsed and I was shattered. My friends thought I was enlightened and I was also under the same illusion, only to witness it falling apart.

Similar experiences happened to a lot of students who sat with my teacher, Papaji. He declared that everybody who had an epiphany was enlightened. If your teacher says this, why not believe it? Only after a few days or a longer period, did they realize that it just was an experience and like every experience, it ended.

Later, Papaji said that in fact none of his students were enlightened, but he told them that because it was better to feel enlightened than not enlightened. When we visited Papaji, he declared my wife enlightened and somehow, I think she was in that state for a day, but then, well, she became her old self once again.

Some teachers even today claim that they became enlightened through Papaji. However, it is not my responsibility to agree or disagree, but only to point out that he was a shaktipat guru (one who can transmit intense spiritual energy for a while in the form of a bliss feeling). He really had no teaching other than "just stop." Certainly for very mature students that might have been just the little push they needed.

Now, back to me and my very personal suffering: I dropped out of meditation, I stopped reading spiritual literature, and I became cynical towards anything spiritual. After that extended bliss experience, I was lost. It took me a while to slowly trust again in teachers. When I finally did it, there was no way to fall back into ignorance and despair.

Sarvakalpa Samadhi VS Nirvikalpa Samadhi

What I experienced above was called sarvakalpa samadhi, a samadhi with seed. The seed was that I was aware of what was happening in my mind. Insights came up and my intellect wanted to make sense of them. This samadhi often comes with a lot of emotional charge, because the jiva does not lose its identity, but only "expands" into atman (the Self - Awareness).

In sarvakalpa samadhi the mind is only conscious of what happens internally and not conscious of the external world. Once this state stabilizes, the meditator might start believing that this state will be permanent. As we should know by now, all experiences disappear.

Any experience is a dualistic appearance in your mind, the Self and you, as an experiencer.

Nirvikalpa samadhi, on the other hand, is absorption without self-consciousness, there is no seed. There is a mergence of the mental activity into the Self to such a degree that the distinction of the knower, the act of knowing, and the object known - dissolves - just as waves vanish into the ocean.

When you enter nirvikalpa samadhi there will not be a memory of what had happened. With no memory of the experience, you cannot extract knowledge from it. The positive side is that vasanas can be neutralized with this type of experience.

Why do we Meditate?

We all have heard the benefits of meditation: a clearer mind, a more relaxed outlook on life, and various health benefits. These days mindfulness is the new buzz word. It refers to the idea that you have to try to stay "present" all the time, and then your life will be peaceful.

Let's examine this idea. Yes, it is true that just by observing the fluctuations of your mind, it will slow down your mind and your breath. This helps to clarify the contents of your mind, including your fears and desires.

The practice of meditation is an effort that cannot sustain a permanent state of calmness by itself. When are you not present? In other words, when is the light of Awareness not shinning? Right, it shines in all three states: waking, sleeping, and dreaming.

So why is meditation not working permanently? Effort, in this case concentration, will have to be given up at one stage. When this happens, suppressed thoughts will rush in again.

It is not enough just to calm your mind, as good as it might feel. First, you need to understand your mind and the process involved in creating thoughts. Just sitting motionless will not produce wisdom. A sattvic state in the mind will produce a pleasant feeling, but it cannot bring knowledge. From where do you think this knowledge will come?

We understand our environment through our senses: we see, we hear, we smell - the eyes, the ears, the nose - are our means of knowledge. To understand the reality of who You are, as the Self, we need another form of perception. We need another means of knowledge. This knowledge is counter intuitive. This means that, at first, it does not make sense. We need an open mind, a trained intellect, and a teacher to clarify the teachings.

Just sitting and watching your breath - or practicing any other form of concentration - will not do it. A silent transmission does not reap understanding either.

Silence is not against ignorance!

Silence is not a teaching, even though sages like Ramana Maharishi used silence to create a space for knowledge to enter the mind. For most of us, just receiving the look of a master will not set us free. We need to "work" to remove our ignorance. Sorry, you may not like to hear this!

Even after sitting for hours, once the effort of watching the mind is over, even the greatest meditator will have to eat, or go to the to the toilet, and the mind inevitably will return with all its force.

There is one more difficulty.

In every meditation practice there are three factors: the watcher, the watched, and the light of Awareness that shines on the meditator. The scriptures tell us that we are living in a non-dual reality, therefore the meditator will have to dissolve the inner duality (watcher/watched) that has been created through meditation. This cannot happen when the focus is on the objects, but rather on the I (the Self, I, as Awareness). Doing this you might feel that your sense of self "falls" deeper into the right side of your chest (Ramana said that this is your spiritual center). Of course You are everywhere, but it could be felt this way.

If you remain identified as the meditator, a practice that is encouraged in Buddhism, duality will remain and you will never know the wholeness and fullness of your being.

Patanjali refers to concentration as the continuous flow of attention towards a single object. That object can be internal, like a visualization of the heart or the third eye, or it can be external, like a yantra or a mandala. Patanjali also mentioned using the stars or the moon as drishtis (focal points). Anything static can become your focal point or anchor, as I like to call it. Whenever your mind is moving into the past or future, you can gently bring it back to your anchor.

Mind is always in the past or in the future because, in the present, it cannot function. The mind needs time and space, which are not found in the continuous present of your being.

After the practice of restraining your mind, the fluctuations will slowly become less, and the very peace and calmness of your being will shine forth. The more you practice it, the more your mind will learn not to be the main player in your life, but rather a servant.

I compare the mind to a puppy dog. In the beginning it seems impossible to tame, you have to repeat orders with the same loving attitude you used the first time. Shouting or getting annoyed will only scare the little puppy. After a while, depending on the receptiveness of the animal, it will learn and obey. Finally the puppy is happy and so are you.

Let's look into meditation and its use for a student of Vedanta. We explained already that meditation is gained through concentration. In Vedanta we use this qualified mind to go into self-inquiry.

Self- inquiry is just the application of knowledge. Self-Inquiry states that Awareness is our true nature and both (knowledge and ignorance) are objects appearing in You, Awareness. This knowledge must be continually contemplated. This is not a meditation, it is the practice of self-inquiry. You train your mind to be single-focused, and after you let it reflect on the truth of your being (nididhyasana).

Self-inquiry is a "higher state" than meditation because the doer, the apparent You, does not need to "do" anything to maintain a particular state and wait for (hopefully) knowledge. You have the knowledge already and you are applying it continually.

Most of the meditators don't value knowledge and somehow they think that it will descend on them. That was exactly what I thought in long meditation retreats and when the samadhi appeared, I was not able to integrate the experience.

Knowledge may arise in meditation or it may not. Even if in your meditation practice some understandings arise, but the knowledge does not always stick. This can leave the meditator frustrated, as he or she will not see any progress.

Concentration

"The difference between an ordinary person and a great person is the degree of concentration." (Swami Vivekananda)

To start practicing meditation we have to understand what concentration (dharana) means and why it is so difficult in the beginning.

One swami said that spirituality is closing your eyes, finding peace, and opening your eyes and asking, "What can I do to help?"

We do just the opposite, we are closing our eyes and finding nothing but confusion and irritation. When we open our eyes we are asking, "What can you do for me?" In order to focus and concentrate it is very helpful to study the Yoga Sutras of Patanjali. He instructs us to get our outer life in order through the observance of the yamas and niyamas and then teaches us to find inner and outer focus points (drishtis) to reach a higher level of concentration that might lead into samadhi.

The west, especially with the development of positive psychology, has embraced that concept and called it "flow." Flow happens through a combination of challenge and skill.

When you start a new task, like learning tennis, you just practice to hit the ball back. After a while, you will learn how to serve the ball into the opposite field, and once you know how to do this, you will start your first game. Each time raising the level of challenge and skill.

Flow is the recognition that challenge and skill are in harmony, boredom means that they are not.

Our mind can be disturbed through our thoughts of selfishness and self-interests. Thinking about your own interests makes you tense and your mind becomes restless, losing its ability to concentrate. An unselfish mind relaxes. It can easily focus. A mind that is focused on love, and a mind that is directed to something higher than your personal concerns is easily focused. It can be focused to your society in the form of service, or to the divine in the form of bhakti.

The quality of your mind is determined by two aspects: how much you can concentrate and what you are concentrating on.

"The mind in its own place makes a heaven of hell and hell of heaven." (From Paradise Lost by John Milton)

After you master the art of concentration, it will become effortless. Once you realize the oneness of your own "small" self with the universal Self, concentration will transform into meditation.

Mediation will also dissolve in the peace that is beyond comprehension: ananta, a fullness and completion where nothing can be added or taken away from you. That was always your true reality, but you were busy looking elsewhere.

16

ENLIGHTENMENT MYTHS

From the very beginning I was fascinated and intrigued by the word "enlightenment."

With no idea what enlightenment meant, I projected that Jesus, Buddha, or Lao-Tzu were enlightened, so it was impossible for me to get there. I had also heard enlightenment stories from modern teachers about light descending, a thousand suns exploding, and other amazing stories of mind-shattering experiences. Consequently these people were "not there anymore" as they had "died and reborn." Their minds had stopped and suddenly they became holier than me, and I was in awe.

Like in any story, there is often a grain of truth in it. Yet a lot is left to the poetic fantasy of the teacher.

Here we will discuss a few myths I have encountered while studying with my teacher, James Swartz.

No Mind or an Empty Mind

When I was practicing zen meditation, this concept was apparently the main focus. Just become "empty" so the divine can fill you. The truth is that we do need a mind because without it would not be possible to comprehend what you are reading. The mind, which is just thoughts, is never the problem.

Certainly there is always some truth in these statements. Once you understand that thoughts are just your vasanas mixed with whatever guna dominates your mind, you don't take them so seriously anymore. However, the mind does not stay "empty," rather you understand that you are not the mind, nor your feelings.

When you don't give them great attention, they move into the background. When this happens, the fluctuations of the mind slow down. You create a space within yourself where thoughts, more connected with the truth of who you are, come to the surface. This cultivates a peaceful, sattvic state of mind, but not enlightenment.

No Ego

This concept suggests that your ego will disappear. A teacher once confronted me with the question, "show me your ego, where is it?"

Obviously you can't show your ego to anybody because it does not exist apart from your idea that it is there, and it seems to define you. This idea is close to the "empty mind" myth. Now it is suggested that an enlightened being has no sense of his individual identity (jiva), implying that they are "not here" - another wrong idea.

The guru with the far away eyes or the teacher who "spaces out" are not an indication of any higher spiritual achievement. Once you actually understand what moksha (enlightenment, freedom) means, you don't fall for this spiritual circus anymore.

You are very much here, where else you can be? The ego, again, is not the problem. The identification with the idea that you are a separate self makes your actions constantly underlined by this fear of separation, which makes you suffer. Yogis call this state avidya (ignorance).

What do you need when you are ignorant? Knowledge (vidya).

There is nothing that dies, and through understanding, you realize that this ego was never real, or as real as a paper tiger. It may be frightening when you see the tiger at first, but once you realize its true nature, you can blow it over.

The ego does not die because it was unreal from the beginning. It only survived because you believed it to be real.

The Power of Now, According to Eckhart Tolle

Here we have something very tempting, and like all beliefs, it has a bit of truth in it. We know that the past is gone and that the future can only be a projection of what you have already understood from past actions.

The future has not happened and it will never happen. When it does, it will be the present moment.

We learned in school that for something to exist in this world, it needs time and space. What about the "now?" Is it in time and space? No, it is not. Is "now" another dimension of time? The word is misleading. When are you not in the "now?" When are you not aware? Apparently, the enlightened person should be always in the "now," big deal, so are you!

When you have your eyes open, you are aware of the stimulus your senses and your mind are giving you. When your eyes are closed, your senses turn inwards and you are more influenced by thoughts and feelings.

The light of Awareness continues to shine undisturbed, just the objects change. If we exchange the "now" with Awareness, then we are on the right track.

The Experience of Oneness

Vedanta states that you are already whole and complete (One), so you don't need an experience of Oneness.

Who will have that experience of Oneness? The Self cannot be experienced, because that is duality.

The Self is the light that is always shining, in which experiences can apparently arise and dissolve.

In a non-dual Existence experiences are unnecessary for liberation because they all assume a form of duality: you and what you are experiencing. Remember, what is the essence of any experience? That it has a beginning, a middle, and an end, and that it cannot be repeated, even though you might want to do that if it was pleasant.

It is all You, just like water is in a wave in the ocean, it is all the same water. It is Awareness appearing apparently in different forms. The wave seems to have an independent reality, but it comes from the ocean and goes back to the ocean and was never separated from it.

Be careful with the language of experience. Enlightenment is not an experience. Enlightenment is the firm knowledge that You are the non-dual, uncreated, limitless, actionless, ordinary Awareness.

Enlightenment is Bliss

This concept doesn't mean that Awareness is blissful. Bliss means that you stop suffering because there are no more fears or egoistical desires. You know you are whole and complete, so there is nothing that can be added or subtracted from you.

Bliss is created by the relationship between Awareness and your body and mind, it does not belong to either of them. Enlightenment is not an achievement. If you are wearing very tight shoes and you remove them, you feel good because the pain is gone, not because you are now barefoot.

Fulfillment of all Your Desires

This concept refers to the idea that some people think that becoming enlightened means that all your desires, especially in regards to money, sex, and power - will be fulfilled. Sorry to disappoint you, but this will not happen. Even though enlightenment is not experiential, it does improve your experience. What you experience after enlightenment is not different to what you were experiencing before.

Remember this famous Zen saying which sums up this point: "Before enlightenment chop wood and carry water, after enlightenment chop wood and carry water."

Another great Zen saying that acknowledges the unsettling nature of this realization is, "First there is a mountain, then there is no mountain anymore. And then there is a mountain again."

What do you think would happen if all of your desires were fulfilled? If you had all the money and appreciation that you desire, what would happen?

What would happen is that the vasanas that were still embedded within you, would sprout and create big obstacles, undermining your inner peace. It is not your desires that need to be fulfilled, they need to be understood and then neutralized in the light of Vedanta: You are already whole and complete.

What is Enlightenment?

It is important that we get a realistic idea of what freedom, moksha, liberation, or enlightenment actually means. If we don't understand it, we can get sucked into the various strange spiritual notions that are out in the spiritual market place.

A related myth about enlightenment is the idea of shaktipat, which is the transference of spiritual energy from teacher to student. As we know by now, you are already what you are looking for, therefore nobody can give you what you already have.

Even more important, if you don't know what you are looking for or have wrong ideas about your goal, you can be easily misled. Yes, it is beautiful to get a blast from a guru, being bathed in light and bliss, but then you return to your seat only to come back to your old sense of being. Subsequently, a vasana for that bliss state will arise in you and you want more and more of it.

Shaktipat is an experience, and if the knowledge of your true Self is not understood, you will become dependent on it. Dependence only creates more pain and disappointment.

In the early days of Osho he used to give shaktipat in his ashram. All the lights were turned off in the room with the exception of a bit of light around him. The disciples came for their "bliss hit."

He stopped this practice after a while because he realized that people stopped meditating, and just waited for their evening "hit" to get through their day. There was fierce competition around who could sit closest to Osho during his satsangs. Sometimes it became hysterical.

I can see the same attitude in modern teachers who support their personal idolization. Be aware that it will only end in tears and not in freedom.

Enlightenment will change your identification with the past. It will disappear, just like the fog after the sun comes through. You will remember it like a story you read.

You understand that you are not extraordinary, you become aware of your utter ordinariness. So if you want to remain special, don't enter the spiritual path. Your ego will not be there to enjoy it!

17

LOVE & RELATIONSHIPS

When we see life as non-dual and the other as the Self, how would that affect our relationships? Knowing that I am Love, how would loving somebody else look like?

Let's step back first and realize that most of the world still connects to another being from a place of need and insecurity.

We don't feel whole and complete, so we think that others can give us that feeling. Logically, you might understand that this is not possible, look at all the heartaches you had. Check if this belief is still working for you. Honesty here is very important. This understanding does not mean that you should separate as soon as you see the dependency.

When you understand Vedanta correctly, you will know that nothing can make you whole and complete because you are it already. But that does not mean that you should not enjoy sharing your life with somebody else, you just need to take off your pink glasses and look at reality with a clear vision.

As humans, we want community and people around us who share our vision of life, so why is there so much misery in a lot of relationships?

Many books have been written about love and relationships. My comments are meant to be read with Vedanta in mind, and not as a self-help book.

The main reason for all strife in life is avidya, which refers to ignorance of our true nature. The ignorance is that we wrongly believe that we are small and incomplete and that we have to beg for love. Nothing could be further from the truth, but without an understanding about the nature of Awareness we will always approach relationships as beggars.

You don't need love because you are love.

All pop songs are misleading: "I need you," I can't live without you," and my favorite, "I want to be your baby tonight." It shows the wrong understanding about love.

The first step in rising in love, rather than falling in love, would be to see each other as whole and independent human beings. You choose to be together not because of need, but because the other can strengthen their own sense of wholeness. This does not mean that you can't compromise, you can. Nothing will be taken away from you. The love you give will be recognized as the love that you are, it never stops flowing.

It will be a joy to make compromises if your partner isn't taking away your freedom to pursue your spiritual path and the relationship is in harmony with dharma.

A deeper level of the relationship will be commitment. This is not a form of dependency, but a form of inner commitment. Your partner is just another expression of Self, and from a spiritual point, you can see the other as a doorway to the divine. It is not so important how the doorframe looks like: big, small, made from wood, or steel, etc. Commitment is strength, assuming the relationship is built on a common vision of dharma.

Moving from partner to partner is a rajasic form of relating, and it will keep the mind busy and excited, rather than calm and contemplative. Therefore it is discouraged for people who want to live a sattvic life.

I personally find relationships (in my case, marriage) very important because nobody can keep you honest like your partner. Living alone can be easy. You can meditate or do other spiritual practices and imagine how developed and "holy" you are. I often joke about this fact: if you want to know if somebody is really liberated, ask the wife or husband of many years!

In a relationship it is necessary to develop qualities like compassion, tolerance, patience, and the ability to go through difficulties together. That is even more true when you have a child. All these qualities are the result of neutralized vasanas. These neutralizations are more difficult to achieve on your own.

18

REINCARNATION

When we look back at the history of humanity, we see that the concept of reincarnation has always been the main belief in many different religions.

For example, in the Bhagavad Gita, Krishna (as the symbol of the Self) lays out clearly the reason for the immortality that you are. He explains that You, as Awareness, were never born. What was not born, cannot die. Therefore, You are always present and unchanging. The body that was born, will eventually dissolve again into where it came from (the five elements).

Let's consider a few more points.

Thoughts are energy. You are able to feel and "perceive" thoughts when you enter a room. If you are entering a sacred place, it "feels" uplifting. You might feel expanded and happy, even though you know that there is nothing in this room that makes you feel that way. The room is only full of "uplifting thought energy." The same is true for scary places.

For example, I have entered holy sites with a shiver of bliss rolling down my spine. On the other hand, when I visited the Dachau Ghetto near Munich with my Jewish wife, I felt physically nauseous. I only looked at the sleeping quarters and the marching ground, but that was enough to trigger these feelings.

Sometimes you just think of a person and then the phone rings. Sometimes you sit close to a loved one, and before you open your mouth they utter something that you just thought of.

If thoughts are energy, then the rule that "energy can't be destroyed" must be true in this case as well. Energy can be directed, transferred or temporally suppressed, but never destroyed. If thoughts can't be destroyed, when the body dies, where do they go? The "thought energy" of desire and fear might find a way to express themselves in a new body. Fears and desires have to be understood by the intellect as just being subconscious tendencies (vasanas). They are ultimately not real.

The science of self-inquiry has similarities with modern science. Microbiology discovered that certain tendencies (the result of ancestor's experiences) are stored in the DNA and passed on to next generations (heredity).

According to genetics the physical traits of parents (tendencies gathered in the DNA) are combined when the sperm fertilizes the egg. They begin to imprint the body of the new individual, determining the development of the fetus, its physical characteristics, and more. Remember, we call them vasanas: the imprints that we are born with.

Vedanta accepts this DNA theory and asks, what is programing the DNA? Logic tells us that it has to be Awareness, what else? Something has to program it.

Would it be so illogical to accept that our fears and desires could be imprinted as well?

If you understood your desires and fears and the fact that objects won't make you happy, you could change your life. You could dissolve your patterns, knowing your immortality as Awareness. If you understand who you are without a shadow of doubt, then no rebirth is necessary or even possible, with only very few exceptions.

Now the bad news! You, as an ego, will vanish. There is no rebirth for an individual personality. What will be reborn are impersonal vasanas and gunas, according to karma. It is better like that!

We need a fresh start as an individual, otherwise life will get too complicated. Knowing all the intricate connections we have had in past lives with our children, parents or friends, would bring us to the brink of madness.

Imagine if you knew that your partner killed you in another life or cheated on you, how would that affect this life?

Every close personal connection you have in this life has karmic patterns originated from past lives. Having said that, sometimes we can get glimpses from a previous life, particularly when there are strong vasanas that still have influences in our life today.

Reincarnation explains something else that confuses a lot of spiritual people. Why do "bad" things happen to "good" people?

If you see life as a flow of consciousness through different bodies, determined by karma (Law of Cause and Effect), it would make sense that nothing is ultimately bad or good. It is just an impersonal unfolding of their vasanas and gunas. There is no injustice, it only appears to us that way because of our limited view.

For example, if you are a parent or if you are around young children, you notice that every child has a different temperament and personality, even before any environmental influences happen. Same parents, same surroundings, yet sometimes very different characters.

There are many beautiful stories of saints who talk about their past lives, like the Buddha for example. He explained to his monks his previous incarnation as a deer or a tiger, and how compassion was common in all his incarnations. Even though I doubt the accuracy of some of the stories, it is still a beautiful poetic thread through the different journeys that the jiva (person) has to go through, before realizing his or her true nature.

Perhaps it would not surprise you that I have had strong memories of past lives. When I was sitting for the first time in Varanasi, a sacred place on the banks of the Ganges, something strange happened.

The red sun was rising over the smoky dust and thousands of pilgrims, including me, were standing waist deep in the water. We were chanting the Gayatri Mantra when something in me just crumbled. It felt like a door opening. A door that allowed me to look into my long past. I knew without a doubt that I have been doing this action, most likely at the same spot, for many, many lifetimes. It felt as if I'd just returned and continuing an action that was a deep vasana in me. I was again a bhakta (devotee of bhakti yoga) and a swami worshipping Surya, the sun, like I must have done many times. My loving wife took me by the hand and led me back to the steps out of the water. I sank my head into her arms and started sobbing for a long time.

The feeling was one of relief, gratitude, and recognition. Relief, because it confirmed that I followed an ancient calling. Gratitude, because of the mysteries unfolding in this life. Recognition, because I had an experiential understanding of the theory of reincarnation.

If you believe that we did not come to this life for the first time, but that consciousness "apparently" evolves through different bodies, then reincarnation makes sense. I say "apparently" because Awareness is already whole and complete, and it cannot go through any evolution. We have to compromise with words because words are not the best vehicle to explain the non-dual reality.

Remember that your actions matter! Every action has a reaction, and it will sooner or later, catch up with you. For example, if you have unresolved issues with your parents, siblings, or ex-partners - find a way to resolve them. It is your energetic connection with them that matters. You can "release" them energetically, even if they are not in their bodies or there is no way to sit face to face with them.

What is the way to do this? Forgiveness. Remember that when they hurt you, they did not know what they were doing. Even if you don't believe that, in their "unawareness," they thought that hurting you would be a desired outcome for them.

Ahimsa (the rule of non-violence, non- hurting in body and mind) is the primordial rule: don't do to others what you don't want for yourself. Violating this will have consequences.

A lot of students ask me what their past lives might have been and my answer is always, " Look at your life right now! What values do you have? What is dear to you?" Go deep into the "heart space" and rediscover. As the Buddhists say, "Samma Sathi," which means, remember rightly. The answer is there.

19

ASHTAVAKRA GITA

I thought a lot about whether I wanted to include this beautiful gita (song) in this book. It summarizes all the important points of Vedanta in a poetic form. And I just love it. I hope you can share my joy in these verses from chapter one. If you would like to read the whole Ashtavakra Gita, please go to Thomas Byron's book, "The Heart of Awareness." Please note that my commentary here is just a guideline. As I said earlier, I am not a Vedantic scholar, but I am just in love with Advaita Vedanta and I want to share it.

First, I want to tell you a bit of the history of this Gita. We know very little about Ashtavakra and we cannot even say that he ever lived. Maybe he was just an invention of a student of Shri Shankara in the fourteen century, or an invention from another sage around the time of the Bhagavad Gita in the fifth or fourth century BCE. It has all the marks of Shankara's style: purifying Shaivism and directly following the Advaita Vedanta teaching.

This gita (song) is a dialogue between the sage Ashtavakra and King Janaka. The word Ashtavakra means eight limps and it is an indication that this person was crippled in eight places. Janaka was a king mentioned in the Mahabarata as the father of Sita. Ashtavakra was his guru. Even though this gita starts as a dialogue, it later becomes the clear and uncompromised teaching of Ashtavakra.

Chapter One: The Self

> *O Master,*
> *Tell me how to find*
> *Detachment, wisdom, and freedom!*

Janaka asks Ashtvakra this question, and it is already full of meaning. The king surrenders his position of power and becomes a humble student. Janaka is a fully qualified person who asks the right questions. (His maturity will be exposed in the second chapter, when the king actually becomes fully enlightened.) He is a king, so he already knows that material objects will not make him happy and that freedom (moksha) will be found in detachment. Only then he will be able to know the peace within that is beyond understanding.

> *Child,*
> *If you wish to be free,*
> *Shun the poison of the senses.*

Their relationship was a spiritual father and his son. From the very beginning, Ashtavakra makes it clear that the biggest obstacle for liberation is the attachment to the information the senses give us. In the Bhagavad Gita they used the example of a turtle that can withdraw its limbs into its shell. We should turn our senses inwards.

> *Seek the nectar of truth,*
> *Of love and forgiveness,*
> *Simplicity and happiness.*

Here he sets up a practice of cultivating happiness. This practice is also the final stage of Self-knowledge.

Earth, fire and water,
The wind and the sky
You are none of these.
If you wish to be free,
Know you are the Self,
The witness of all these,
The heart of Awareness.

Now this is it! If you understand that you are free of all objects, you can go home and live your life any way you want to.

Set your body aside.
Sit in your own Awareness.
You will at once be happy,
Forever still,
Forever free.
You have no caste.
No duties bind you.
Formless and free,
Beyond the reach of the senses,
The witness of all things.
So be happy!

This Gita is not a teaching manual like the Bhagavad Gita. Rather it celebrates the fruit of knowledge and understanding. He does not tell you why you are not the body, and why you are the witness of this form - formless and free. Standing on the highest point of realization, what else is left? "Be happy." He does not recommend to start sharing with others or create an ashram or an organization, no, just be happy!

Right or wrong,
Joy and sorrow,
These are of the mind only.
They are not yours.

The gita could have stopped here, but lucky for us, it keeps on going. It returns to the same theme again and again, dismantling doubts, if there were any. It is just the overflowing joy that is in Ashtavakra's heart. Right and wrong are only in your mind. Reality is just the way it is, and we put a judgment on it according to our values. Life is unfolding according to the universal plan (Ishvara's will) and it is neither good nor bad. We can just say, "it is the way it is." Joy and sorrow are emotional states that come and go and don't even leave a mark on who we truly are: unchanging Awareness. All is in flux, except You.

It is not really you
Who acts or enjoys.
You are everywhere,
Forever free.
Forever and truly free,
The single witness of all things.

If it is not you, the ego, who suffers and enjoys?

From the highest Vedantic understanding, nobody enjoys or suffers because we live in a non-dual reality. For someone to suffer, there has to be a person and the suffering. Vedanta states that there is no separate person, just an idea of a person. An idea most of us are deeply attached to. You are not the changing apparent person. You are the container of all that is.

But if you see yourself as separate,
Then you are bound.
"I do this. I do that."
The big black snake of selfishness
Has bitten you!

This is the poison! Thinking you need to protect yourself against others. Thinking that it is you against the world, and that you are an island in a vast ocean of suffering. You think you are a doer because you identify with this body and its senses. Vedanta teaches you that "things" are happening and you are not the doer or enjoyer of these actions.

"I do nothing."
This is the nectar of faith,
So drink and be happy!

Faith is a qualification for enlightenment. Remember sravana, manana and nididhyasana: first you have to have faith in what the scriptures are telling you. Then you listen to teachers who can clarify your doubts. Finally, you start practicing what you have heard and your trust will keep growing. We are not talking about blind faith, but faith that is based on your own experience.

Know you are One,
Pure Awareness.
With the fire of this conviction,
Burn down the forest of ignorance.
Free yourself from sorrow,
And be happy.

Sorrow will disappear by itself once you know that you are pure Awareness. Ignorance is like a dark room. Even though the room might have been dark for centuries, one candle makes the darkness effortlessly disappear. Once sorrow is understood to be just ignorance, happiness will follow it like a shadow.

> *Be happy!*
> *For you are joy, unbounded joy.*
> *You are Awareness itself.*

This will be the realization: whatever you were looking for is already within you. You have been looking all over the world, only to realize that it was sitting in the "cave of your heart" all along. Joy, unbound joy, will be the result of this discovery. You are the joy. The joy is not somewhere outside you.

> *Just as a coil of rope*
> *Is mistaken for a snake,*
> *So you are fearful of the world*
> *not knowing the bliss that you are.*

Here we have the famous parable of the snake and the rope:

In the twilight a pilgrim walks into a village and when he is close to a well, he suddenly jumps back in fear. He sees a coiled, big black snake lying on the ground. His fear is real: his heart is pumping, his breath is fast and erratic, and he is standing still, frozen in terror. An old man (representing wisdom) sees him and asks, "Why are you so afraid?" The wanderer points to the coiled snake and trembles. The wise man just laughs and says to the pilgrim, "this is just a coiled rope! On this rope there is a bucket with which we collect water."

There is no need to be afraid. It might look like a snake for the pilgrim, but he just super imposed a snake onto the rope. With the explanation that the wise man gave him, the wanderer was immediately released from his fear. He could see his mistake and started laughing about the real fear he was experiencing a short time ago.

Was the snake real? Yes and no.

It seemed real when he first saw it and his body responded to the seeming fear. Once the rope was recognized, all the fear disappeared but nothing really had changed. Other travelers still might see a snake, but not him. He was freed from his superimposition and could clearly see the rope looking like a snake. He was freed from ignorance.

This is such an old and renowned teaching story. Freedom (moksha) is just like that: nothing really changes, but what was mistaken for a reality is recognized to be just a wrong view. As the Buddhists would say, once the rope is seen as a rope (once reality is seen for what is), all fear disappears.

If you think you are free,
You are free.
If you think you are bound,
You are bound.
For the saying is true:
You are what you think.

Remember this is not to be confused with ideas like "The Secret," even though they use this verse as a confirmation for their naïve ideas. Their thesis is: think about the fulfillment of your desires day in and day out, and it will happen. Of course, you will be just the same greedy person, but maybe with more material possessions. However, nothing would have changed within you. Just the opposite, a vasana for more objects will be created. You will continue to be a slave of your desires, thinking that the joy lies in the possession of objects.

What is meant here is that thoughts are very powerful, and they can be used for liberation rather than for self-destruction . Reality is the way it is, neither good nor bad, but our thinking makes it one way or another.

"The most important decision we make is whether we believe we live in a friendly or hostile universe." (Albert Einstein)

Positive thoughts can lift you up and negative thoughts will pull you down. I think you all know this by now. But a thought is just that, an energetic pattern that came from a combination of the guna that was operating at the time, and the vasana that was triggered. There was no choice from your side, and only when the thought is recognized by Awareness, you can have some control over it.

This is the conclusion we find in the Ashtavakra Gita: "Don't let your thinking dictate who you are." See a thought for what it is and then either ignore it and focus on something else, or try to counter act it with a positive thought.

What is a positive thought?

"I am - as the Self - non-dual, actionless, uncreated, unlimited, ordinary Awareness." This is what I really am, and not other self-destructing thoughts. It is best to let them go, and focus on what the reality of my being truly is. In the beginning that might sound fake, yet try it and see for yourself. It does work because it is the truth. There is a saying in the Bible: "The truth will set you free."

The Self looks like the world.
But this is just an illusion.
The Self is everywhere.

Remember the metaphorical explanation we find in the scriptures about spiders and their webs. It says that the world is for us what the spider web is to the spider. Is the spider web part of the spider? Yes. Could the spider web exist without the spider? No, but spiders can be without webs. The spider web is created by the spider. It will dissolve one day, but the spider will continue to exist.

From the Self, the world is created. It will dissolve one day, back into the Self. The world is dependent on the Self for its very existence - but the Self - pure Awareness, can be without a world.

As Ramana Maharishi said: " The Self does not move, the world moves in it."

One.
Still.
Free.
Perfect.
The witness of all things,
Awareness
Without action, clinging or desire.

Knowing this is important, but you have to actualize it in your daily life. This means living your life from the standpoint of Awareness, and not falling into old patterns.

Meditate on the Self.
One without two,
Exalted Awareness.
Give up the illusion
Of the separate self.

Here he points to the right way to meditate. Being mindful of your breath is the first step. After that you have to move beyond the dualistic view of observer and observed, and go straight to the essence of who you really are, the one without a second. Here the dualistic view merges in the non-dualistic reality of Advaita Vedanta.

As Ramakrishna said: "See God everywhere, not only when you close your eyes."

> *Give up the feeling*
> *Within or without,*
> *That you are this or that.*

You cannot point to what you are, you just are!

As my teacher James often says: "I am the space-like [Awareness] in which all bodies appear, including the one I think is mine."

> *My child,*
> *Because you think you are the body,*
> *For a long time you have been bound.*
> *Know you are pure Awareness.*
> *With this knowledge as your sword*
> *Cut through your chains.*
> *And be happy!*

The identification with the body is the first and often the hardest to give up: we identify the information the senses give us with who we are. This body-mind complex is deeply rooted in us, and Vedanta seems counter intuitive.

For you are already free,
Without action or flaw,
Luminous and bright.
You are bound
Only by the habit of meditation
Your nature is pure Awareness
You are flowing in all things,
And all things are flowing in you.
But beware
The narrowness of the mind!
You are always the same,
Unfathomable Awareness,
Limitless and free,
Serene and unperturbed.
Desire only your own Awareness.
Whatever takes form is false.
Only the formless endures.
When you understand
The truth of this teaching,
You will not be born again.
For God is infinite,
Within the body and without,
Like a mirror,
And the image in a mirror.
As the air is everywhere,
Flowing around a pot
And filling it,
So God is everywhere,
Filling all things
And flowing through them forever.

Attachment to seeking keeps one in bondage. Seeking stops once your true nature is revealed. You will realize that you are already what you were looking for. Separation is only a wrong idea. You are the world and the world is You.

Mind is afraid to lose its hold on you. You are always the same, pure Awareness, flowing in all directions. The mind, with its narrow identification, is a powerful foe. The mind is limited, you are not! There should be only one desire: to be free or to know who you are, which are the same thing.

Awareness was never born. Everything that was/is born will have to disappear one day. What is never born cannot disappear. It is said in the Upanishads: "Tat Tvam Asi." Translation: You are That.

There will not be any karmic ignorance or desire that will want or need another body. You know that you are essentially unborn.

If we say that the pot is made of clay, God is the clay and the pot is the creation. You are aware of both. You are the essence of everything. Nothing exists without you.

Happiness will spring forth without effort or maintenance once this has been realized.

Hari Om Tat Sat

20

VEDANTA CHARTS

Here we have a visual "roadmap" to the teachings of Advaita Vedanta in an informal and humorous way.

Is important not to become too serious when discussing these teachings. Maybe some Sanskrit scholars can even feel disturbed by the way we are sharing these teachings here. Sorry, we are just trying to reach "ordinary people" who could benefit tremendously with this knowledge. We really believe that it can save them from suffering and avoid the waste of time with the misleading teachings that are there in the spiritual market place.

THE 10 CHARTS

1. The essence of Advaita Vedanta
2. Samsara
3. Freedom
4. Satya/Mithya
5. The 3 buckets teaching 1
6. The 3 buckets teaching 2
7. Karma yoga
8. Mandukya Upanishad
9. Qualifications
10. Vedanta's rockstars

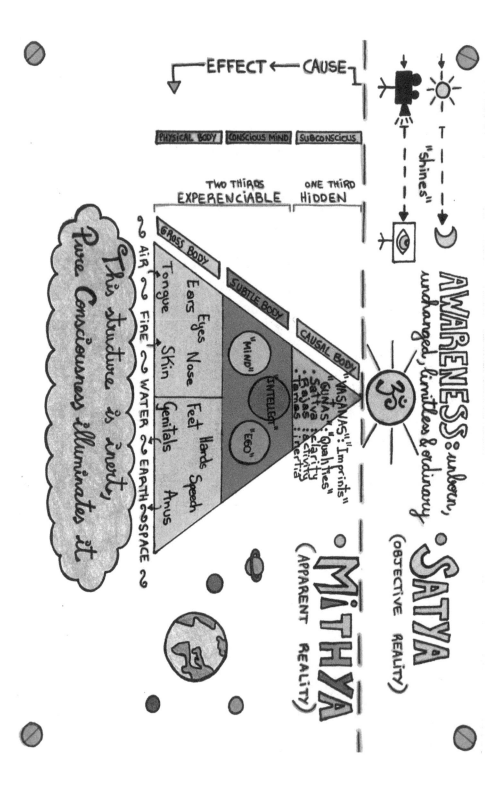

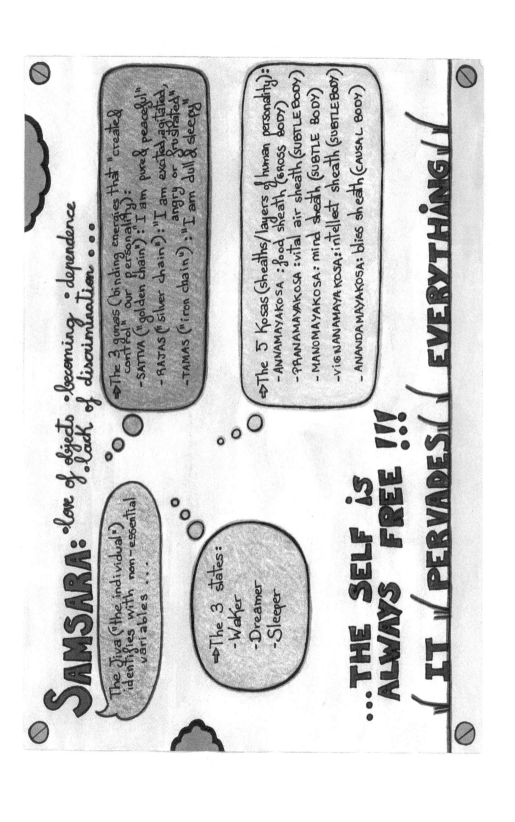

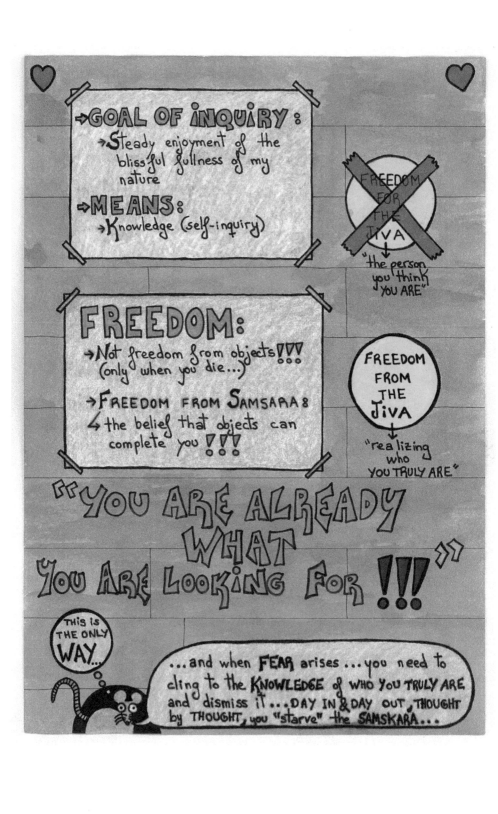

SATYA (objective reality / never changes)

MITHYA (apparted reality / keeps changing)

CONSCIOUSNESS = EXISTENCE = AWARENESS = THE SELF ∘∘∘

: The world of objects, the individual, all the names &

forms & transactions that "occur" in Awareness ...

AWARENESS + THOUGHT = EXPERIENCE

AWARENESS + SUBTLE BODY = JIVA ⟨ tree / human ⟩ } "reflecting Awareness"

AWARENESS + GROSS BODY = MATTER } "absorbent matter, not reflecting Awareness"

"Everything is Awareness ... all pervasive, limitless, unchanged, unborn, ... "

→ The 3 buckets teaching : "THE THREE GUNAS" (PART 1)

SATYA ─┐ OBJECTIVE REALITY │ THAT WHICH NEVER CHANGES
MITHYA │ APPARENT REALITY │ THAT WHICH KEEPS CHANGING

ॐ

- Samskaras + Gunas Initiated
- Mind Ego
- 5 elements

Tendencies/imprints
3 "qualities/energies" that "colour" our personality

"subconscious" → CAUSAL BODY
"conscious mind" → SUBTLE BODY
"physical body" → GROSS BODY

→ VEDANTA IS THE SCIENCE OF THE SELF : Through Self-Inquiry we "prepare" the Subtle Body → managing/neutralizing binding LIKES & DISLIKES
"chain" me to experience
all experience is in SAMSARA & subject to change

→ THE GUNAS CONTROL EXPERIENCE

→ "THE SUN SHINES" in "3 buckets" :

ॐ

PROBLEM

① BUCKET WITH CLEAR/PRISTINE WATER

② BUCKET WITH SCATTERED/CHOPPY WATER

③ BUCKET WITH MUDDY/MURKY WATER

a) Bucket 1 Sattva : Mode of Knowledge & bliss. Feeling of bliss. Feeling of "no movement", feeling "in the zone". Strong value for renunciation & dispassion, love of spiritual culture, humility....

b) Bucket 2 Rajas : Mode of Passion. Feeling of low restless dissatisfied energy. Keeps the mind & emotions perpetually disturbed. Ego oriented : high when you get what you want, frustrated when you don't....

c) Bucket 3 Tamas : Mode of inertia & dullness. Feeling of stuckness, cloudy energy. Keeps the mind confused, with a sense of failure & depression....

→ The 3 buckets teaching: "THE THREE GUNAS" (PART 2)

QUESTION

→ The Sun (The Self/Consciousness/Awareness) shines on the 3 buckets
(the 3 gunas: Sattva, Rajas, Tamas)... which bucket will
reflect the Sun better ???

ANSWER

→ Bucket 1 (Sattva) reflects better, like a clean mirror...

"SPIRITUAL GROWTH NEEDS PROPPER ASSIMILATION

OF EXPERIENCE, WHICH HAPPENS ONLY WHEN

THE "MIND" (SUBTLE BODY) IS ALERT & PRESENT:

These are Sattvic Qualities"

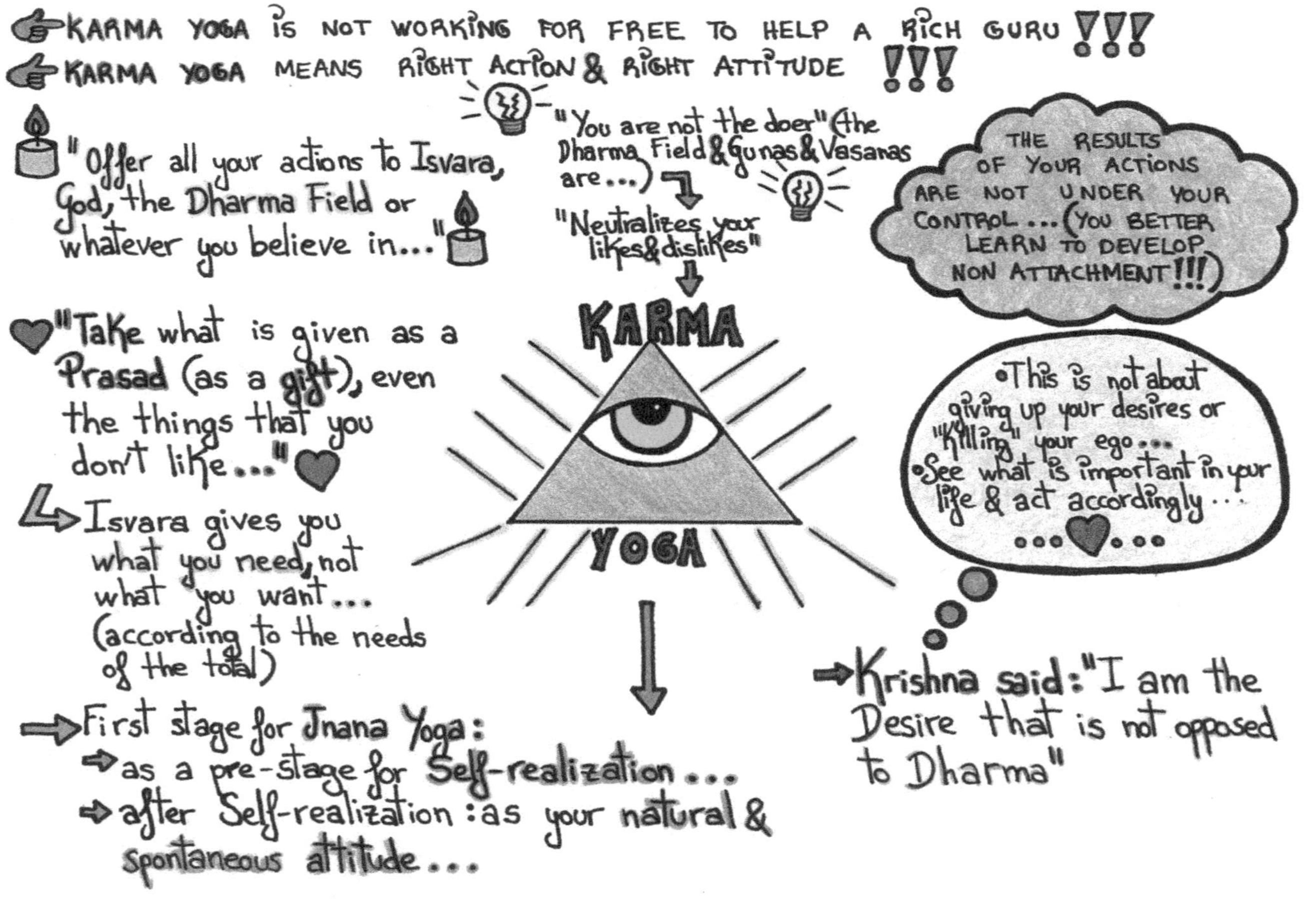
KARMA YOGA IS NOT WORKING FOR FREE TO HELP A RICH GURU !!!
KARMA YOGA MEANS RIGHT ACTION & RIGHT ATTITUDE !!!
"Offer all your actions to Isvara, God, the Dharma Field or whatever you believe in..."
"You are not the doer" (the Dharma Field & Gunas & Vasanas are...)
"Neutralizes your likes & dislikes"
THE RESULTS OF YOUR ACTIONS ARE NOT UNDER YOUR CONTROL... (YOU BETTER LEARN TO DEVELOP NON ATTACHMENT!!!)
"Take what is given as a Prasad (as a gift), even the things that you don't like..."
KARMA
YOGA
•This is not about giving up your desires or "Killing" your ego...
•See what is important in your life & act accordingly...
Isvara gives you what you need, not what you want... (according to the needs of the total)
Krishna said: "I am the Desire that is not opposed to Dharma"
First stage for Jnana Yoga:
as a pre-stage for Self-realization...
after Self-realization: as your natural & spontaneous attitude...

Mandukya Upanishad

→ 3 experiencing entities:

- the shortest one (only 12 verses)
- "the whole Cosmos is the word **AUM**"
- "Frog Upanishad": the Self "jumps" from one state to the other

3ॐ
"formless Consciousness"

③ THE SLEEPER

Sense organs
EGO
MIND
INTELLECT
3ॐ
"Consciousness turned outward"

① THE WAKER

Sense organs
EGO
MIND
INTELLECT
3ॐ
"Consciousness turned inward"

② THE DREAMER

① THE WAKER: as a "consumer of experience"; the Vasanas are expressed as thoughts & feelings

② THE DREAMER: as "the shining one"; Awareness illumines the Vasanas playing out as images on the screen

③ THE SLEEPER: as a "mass of Consciousness"; like a seed state where the Vasanas are dormant

∞ "If I AM REAL, I have to exist ALL THE TIME" (in the 3 states) ∞

from the **GOLD**, you can create rings, bracelets, ... → the SELF is the
from the **CLAY**, you can create pots, plates, ...   GOLD/CLAY

QUALIFICATIONS:

1) **VIVEKA:** discrimination between the eternal & non-eternal
2) **VAIRAGYA:** dispassion for the non-eternal
3) **6 DISCIPLINES** FOR THE **MIND:**
   - calmness of the mind
   - control of the sense organs
   - detachment from worldly enjoyments
   - contentment
   - spiritual courage
   - faith
4) **MUMUKSHUTVA:** intense desire for liberation

...ARE YOU READY FOR VEDANTA?

VEDANTA'S ROCKSTARS

ADI SHANKARACHARYA
(788 CE - 820 CE)

"Brahman is the only truth, the world is an illusion, and there is ultimately no difference between Brahman and the individual Self"

SWAMI CHINMAYANANDA
(1916 - 1993)

"Moksha is not Freedom from action, but Freedom in action"

SWAMI SARVAPRIYANANDA
(1973 - ...)

"We are this Consciousness. It is a statement of fact. It is true for all of us"

RAMANA MAHARSHI
(1879 - 1950)

"We imagine that we will realize the Self sometime, whereas we are anything but the Self"

JAMES SWARTZ
(1941 - ...)

"I am whole & complete, actionless, unborn, limitless, ordinary Awareness"

SWAMI VIVEKANANDA
(1893 - 1902)

"The dry & abstract Advaita must become living & poetic in everyday life"

SWAMI DAYANANDA
(1930 - 2015)

"It is not wrong to be ignorant. It is an error to continue to be ignorant"

21

SANSKRIT GLOSSARY

Adharma: Behavior that is contrary to the natural and moral order.

Advaita: Non-dual. Not two.

Ahamkara: Ego, the "I" notion.

Ajnana: Ignorance, in the context of Vedanta, ignorance of one's self as Awareness.

Ananda: Bliss, fullness.

Annamaya Kosha: The food sheath, the gross body.

Apana: Power in the pranayama kosha.

Ashram: A spiritual hermitage or monastery in Indian religions.

Atma: The Self.

Atmananda: The bliss of the Self.

Avidya: Personal ignorance of the Self.

Bhakti: Worship, devotion.

Brahman: The limitless Self when referred to as the essence of creation.

Brahmananda: The bliss of Awareness.

Buddhi: Intellect, the discriminating function.

Chit: Awareness, the inner immortal essence of every individual, also called the Self.

Dharana: Concentration in yoga philosophy. In Vedanta, a steady mind cultivated by the realization of the Self in every thought.

Gunas: The 3 qualities or energies that shape and modify our personality.

Jnana Yoga: the yoga of knowledge.

Jiva: a living being, any entity with life force.

Karma: action, the Law of Cause and Effect.

Mañana: The second stage of inquiring. Bringing the new understanding in your life and discarding the old assumptions.

Manomaya Kosha: The mind sheath; the doubting mind, the emotional function.

Mantra: Sacred revealing words, typically chanted in repetition.

Maya: Ignorance; a power dependent on the Self that makes creation possible, composed of the three gunas. It is neither the same as the Self nor is it different from the Self.

Mithya: That which is apparently real. The objects, gross and subtle, that appear in Awareness.

Moksha: Liberation, freedom.

Mumukshutva: Burning desire for freedom, a primary qualification for inquiry.

Nama: Name.

Nididhyasana: The third stage of inquiry: assimilation, dwelling on the teachings.

Nirguna: Without properties or qualities.

Nirvana: A thought-free mind in which there is no sense of a separate Self.

Nirvikalpa: Non-dual. Free of thoughts, differences, division.

Nirvikalpa samadhi: A state of pure, objectless experience and knowledge. A state in which all sheaths, including the bliss sheath, are absent. A state of total absorption in the Self.

Niyama: Individual observances, as explained in the Patanjali Yoga Sutras.

Pranamaya kosha ; The energy sheath composed of prana; the vital shell of the body that contains life. The existence of pranamaya kosha is what differentiates the living from the dead.

Prakriti: Nature, the substance from which all objects evolve.

Purusha: Universal principle that is unchanging.

Rajas: Guna characterized by activity and passion.

Sadhana: A spiritual practice.

Samanya Dharma: Moral laws that govern the field of existence.

Samskara: Deep imprints (vasanas) in our subconscious mind (causal body).

Sattva: Guna characterized by peace and clarity.

Shanti: Peace.

Sravana: The first stage of inquiry: systematic unfolding, hearing and understanding with an open, non-judgmental mind.

Sruti: That which is heard, scriptures in Vedic literature.

Svadharma: Doing one's God-given duty.

Tamas: Guna characterized by inertia and dullness.

Tat Tvam Asi: "You are That," referring to the identity of the Self and the jiva.

Udana: Power of the Pranamaya Kosha.

Vairagya: Dispassion, one of the qualifications for inquiry.

Vasana: Imprints, subtle impressions produced by actions that are stored in the causal body, and will produce more actions.

Vidya: Knowledge.

Vijgnanamaya Kosha: The intellect sheath and the organs of perception, the discriminating function (buddhi).

Viveka: Discrimination, not confusing the Self with the objects appearing in it.

Vyana: Power of Pranamaya Kosha.

Visesa Dharma: Individual interpretation of the moral laws that govern the field of existence.

Yama: Social observances.

Yoga: To join or yoke. In Vedanta: the complete absorption of the mind in the thought "I am Awareness and not the body-mind-sense complex."

About the Authors

Stephan Kahlert (Pujan) is a meditation and philosophy teacher, facilitator, and therapist who lives with his wife in Thailand. He has been teaching and lecturing for over 30 years around the world.

Sole has been involved in education and social projects - from her home country of Spain to India - where she also studied yoga and Vedanta. She loves to bring Art and Vedanta together.

Lightning Source UK Ltd.
Milton Keynes UK
UKHW021330201020
371853UK00007B/434